THE SELECTED WORKS OF

Anicius Manlius Severinus Boethius

Including
THE TRINITY IS ONE GOD NOT THREE GODS
And
CONSOLATION OF PHILOSOPHY

© 2010 Benediction Classics.

THE TRINITY IS ONE GOD NOT THREE GODS

A TREATISE BY

ANICIUS MANLIUS SEVERINUS BOETHIUS

MOST HONOURABLE, OF THE ILLUSTRIOUS ORDER OF EX-CONSULS, PATRICIAN TO HIS FATHER-IN-LAW, QUINTUS AURELIUS MEMMIUS SYMMACHUS MOST HONOURABLE, OF THE ILLUSTRIOUS ORDER OF EX-CONSULS, PATRICIAN

NOTE ON THE TEXT

IN preparing the text of the Consolatio I have used the apparatus in Peiper's edition (Teubner, 1871), since his reports, as I know in the case of the Tegernseensis, are generally accurate and complete; I have depended also on my own collations or excerpts from various of the important manuscripts, nearly all of which I have at least examined, and I have also followed, not always but usually, the opinions of Engelbrecht in his admirable article, Die Consolatio Philosophiae des Boethius in the Sitzungsberichte of the Vienna Academy, cxliv. (1902) 1-60. The present text, then, has been constructed from only part of the material with which an editor should reckon, though the reader may at least assume that every reading in the text has, unless otherwise stated, the authority of some manuscript of the ninth or tenth century; in certain orthographical details, evidence from the text of the Opuscula Sacra has been used without special mention of this fact. We look to August Engelbrecht for the first critical edition of the Consolatio at, we hope, no distant date.

The text of the Opuscula Sacra is based on my own collations of all the important manuscripts of these works. An edition with complete apparatus criticis will be ready before long for the Vienna corpis Scriptorum Ecclesiasticorum Latinorum. The history of the text of the Opuscula Sacra, as I shall attempt to show elsewhere, is intimately connected with that of the Consolatio.

E. K. R.

INTRODUCTION

ANICIUS MANLIUS SEVERINUS BOETHIUS, of the famous Praenestine family of the Anicii, was born about 480 A.D. in Rome. His father was an ex-consul; he himself was consul under Theodoric the Ostrogoth in 510, and his two sons, children of a great granddaughter of the renowned Q. Aurelius Symmachus, were joint consuls in 522. His public career was splendid and honourable, as befitted a man of his race, attainments, and character. But he fell under the displeasure of Theodoric, and was charged with conspiring to deliver Rome from his rule, and with corresponding treasonably to this end with Justin, Emperor of the East. He was thrown into prison at Pavia, where he wrote the Consolation of Philosophy, and he was as brutally put to death in 524. His brief and busy life was marked by great literary achievement. His learning was vast, his industry untiring, his object unattainable--nothing less than the transmission to his countrymen of all the works of Plato and Aristotle, and the reconciliation of their apparently divergent views. To form the idea was a silent judgment on the learning of his day; to realize it was more than one man could accomplish; but Boethius accomplished much. He translated the E of Porphyry, and the whole of Aristotle's Organon. He wrote a double commentary on the E, and commentaries on the Categories and the De Interpretatione of Aristotle, and on the Topica of Cicero. He also composed original treatises on the categorical and hypothetical syllogism, on Division and on Topical Differences. He adapted the arithmetic of Nicomachus, and his textbook on music, founded on various Greek authorities, was in use at Oxford and Cambridge until modern times. His five theological Tractates are here, together with the Consolation of Philosophy to speak for themselves.

Boethius was the last of the Roman philosophers and the first of the scholastic theologians. The present volume serves to prove the truth of both these assertions.

The Consolation of Philosophy is indeed, as Gibbon called it, "a golden volume, not unworthy of the leisure of Plato or of Tully." To belittle its originality and sincerity, as is sometimes done, with view to saving the Christianity of the writer, is to misunderstand his mind and his method. The Consolatio is not, as has been maintained, a mere patchwork of translations from Aristotle and the Neoplatonists. Rather it is the supreme essay of one who throughout his life had found his highest solace in the dry light of reason. His chief source of refreshment, in the dungeon to which his beloved library had not accompanied him, was a memory well stocked with the poetry and thought of former days. The development of the argument is anything but Neoplatonic; it is all his own.

And if the Consolation of Philosophy admits Boethius to the company of Cicero or even of Plato, the theological Tractates mark him as the forerunner of St. Thomas. It was the habit of a former generation to regard Boethius as an eclectic, the transmitter of a distorted Aristotelianism, a pagan, or at best a luke-warm Christian, who at the end cast off the faith which he had worn in times of peace, and wrapped himself in the philosophic cloak which properly belonged to him. The authenticity of the Tractates was freely denied. We know better now. The discovery by Alfred Holder, and the illuminating discussion by Hermann Usener, [1] of a fragment of Cassiodorus are sufficient confirmation of the manuscript tradition, apart from the work of scholars who have sought to justify that tradition from internal evidence. In that fragment Cassiodorus definitely ascribes to his friend Boethius "a book on the Trinity, some dogmatic chapters, and a book against Nestorius." [2] Boethius was without doubt a Christian, a Doctor and perhaps a martyr. Nor is it necessary to think that, when in prison, he put away his faith. If it is asked why the Consolation of Philosophy contains no conscious or direct reference to the doctrines which are traced in the Tractates with so sure a hand, and is, at most, not out of harmony with Christianity, the answer is simple. In the Consolation he is writing philosophy; in the Tractates he is writing theology. He observes what Pascal calls the orders of things. Philosophy belongs to one order, theology to another. They have different objects. The object of philosophy is to understand and explain the nature of the world around us; the object of theology is to understand and explain doctrines delivered by divine revelation. The scholastics recognized the distinction, [3] and the corresponding difference in the function of Faith and Reason. Their final aim was to co-ordinate the two but this was not possible before the thirteenth century. Meanwhile Boethius helps to prepare the way. In the Consolation he gives Reason her range and suffers her, unaided, to vindicate the ways of Providence. In the Tractates Reason is called in to give to the claims of Faith the support which it does not really lack. [4] Reason, however, has still a right to be heard. The distinction between fides and ratio is proclaimed in the first two Tractates . In the second especially it is drawn with a clearness worthy of St. Thomas himself; and there is, of course the implication that the higher authority resides with fides. But the treatment is philosophical and extremely bold. Boethius comes back to the question of the substantiality of the divine Persons which he has discussed in Tr. I. from a fresh point of view. Once more he decides that the Persons are predicated relatively; even Trinity, he concludes, is not predicated substantially of deity. Does this square with catholic doctrine? It is possible to hear a note of challenge in his words to John the Deacon, fidem si poterit rationemque coniunge. Philosophy states the problem in unequivocal terms. Theology is required to say whether they commend themselves.

One object of the scholastics, anterior to the final con-ordination of the two sciences, was to harmonize and codify all the answers to all the questions that philosophy raises. The ambition of Bonethius was not so soaring, but it was sufficiently bold. He set out, first to translate, and then to reconcile, Plato and Aristotle; to go behind all the other systems, even the latest and the most in vogue, back to the two great masters, and to show that they have the truth, and are in substantial accord. So St. Thomas himself, if he cannot reconcile the teaching of Plato and Aristotle, at least desires to correct the one by the other, to discover what truth is common to both, and to show its correspondence with Christian doctrine. It is reasonable to conjecture that Boethius, if he had lived, might have attempted something of the kind. Were he alive today, he might feel more in tune with the best of the pagans than with most contemporary philosophic thought.

In yet one more respect Boethius belongs to the company of the schoolmen. He not only put into circulation many precious philosophical notions, served as channel through which various works of Aristotle passed into the schools, and handed down to them a definite Aristotelian method for approaching the problem of faith; he also supplied material for that classification of the various sciences which is an essential accompaniment of every philosophical movement, and of which the Middle Ages felt the value. [5] The uniform distribution into natural sciences, mathematics and theology which he recommends may be traced in the work of various teachers up to the thirteenth century, when it is finally accepted and defended by St. Thomas in his commentary on the De Trinitate.

A seventeenth-century translation of the consolatio Philosophiae is here presented with such alterations as are demanded by a better text, and the requirements of modern scholarship. There was, indeed not much to do, for the rendering is most exact. This in a translation of that date is not a little remarkable. We look for fine English and poetry in an Elizabethan; but we do not often get from him such loyalty to the original as is here displayed. Of the author "I. T." nothing is known. He may have been John Thorie, a Fleming born in London in 1568, and a B.A. of Christ Church, 1586. Thorie "was a person well skilled in certain tongues, and a noted poet of his times " (Wood, Athenae Oxon ed. Bliss, i. 624), but his known translations are apparently all from the Spanish.

Our translator dedicates his "Five books on Philosophical Comfort" to the Dowager Countes of Dorset, widow of Thomas Sackville, who was part author of A Mirror for Magistrates and Gorboduc and who, we learn from I. T.'s preface, meditated similar work. I. T. does not unduly flatter h patroness, and he tells her plainly that she will not understand the philosophy of the book, though the theological and practical parts may be within her scope.

The Opuscucla Sacra have never before, to our knowledge, been translated. In reading and rendering them we have been greatly helped by two mediaeval commentaries: one by John the Scot (edited by E. K. Rand in Traube's Quellen und Untersuchungen, vol. i. Pt. 2, Munich, 1906); the other by Gilbert de la Porree (printed in Migne, P.L. lxiv. We also desire to record our indebtedness in many points of scholarship and philosophy to Mr. E. Thomas of Emmanuel College.

H.F.V.

E.K.R.

[1] Anecdoton Holderi, Leipzig, 1877.
[2] Scripsil librum de sancta trinitate et capita quaedam dogmatica et librum contra Nestorium. On the question of the genuineness of Tr. IV. De fide catholica see note ad loc.
[3] Cp. H. de Wulf, Histoire de la Philosophie medieval (Louvain and Paris 1915), p. 332.
[4] See below, De Trin. vi. ad fin.
[5] Cp. L. Baur, Gundissalinus: de divisione, Munster, 1905.

I HAVE long pondered this problem with such mind as I have and all the light that God has lent me. Now, having set it forth in logical order and cast it into literary form, I venture to submit it to your judgment, for which I care as much as for the results of my own research. You will readily understand what I feel whenever I try to write down what I think if you consider the difficulty of the topic and the fact that I discuss it only with the few--I may say with no one but yourself. It is indeed no desire for fame or empty popular applause that prompts my pen; if there be any external reward, we may not look for more warmth in the Verdict than the subject itself arouses. For, a part from yourself, wherever I turn my eyes, they fall on either the apathy of the dullard or the jealousy of the shrewd, and a man who casts his thoughts before the common herd--I will not say to consider but to trample under foot, would seem to bring discredit on the study of divinity. So I purposely use brevity and wrap up the ideas I draw from the deep questionings of philosophy in new and unaccustomed words which speak only to you and to myself, that is, if you deign to look at them. The rest of the world I simply disregard: they cannot understand, and therefore do not deserve to read. We should not of course press our inquiry further than man's wit and reason are allowed to climb the height of heavenly knowledge. [6] In all the liberal arts some limit is set beyond which reason may not reach. Medicine, for instance, does not always bring health to the sick, though the doctor will not be to blame if he has left nothing undone which he ought to do. So with the other arts. In the present case the very difficulty of the quest claims a lenient judgment. You must however examine whether the seeds sown in my mind by St. Augustine's writings [7] have borne fruit. And now let us begin our inquiry.

CHAPTER I.

There are many who claim as theirs the dignity of the Christian religion; but that form of faith is valid and only valid which, both on account of the universal character of the rules and doctrines affirming its authority, and because the worship in which they are expressed has spread throughout the world, is called catholic or universal. The belief of this religion concerning the Unity of the Trinity is as follows: the Father is God, the Son is God, the Holy Spirit is God. Therefore Father, Son, and Holy Spirit are one God, not three Gods. The cause of this union is absence of difference: [8] difference cannot be avoided by those who add to or take from the Unity, as for instance the Arians, who, by graduating the Trinity according to merit, break it up and convert it to Plurality. For the essence of plurality is otherness; apart from otherness plurality is unintelligible. In fact, the difference between three or more things lies in genus or species or number. Difference is the necessary correlative of sameness. Sameness is predicated in three ways: By genus; e.g. a man and a horse, because of their common genus, animal. By species; e.g. Cato and Cicero, because of their common species, man. By number; e.g. Tully and Cicero, because they are one and the same man. Similarly, difference is expressed by genus, species, and number. Now numerical difference is caused by variety of accidents; three men differ neither by genus nor species but by their accidents, for if we mentally remove from them all other accidents, [9] still each one occupies a different place which cannot possibly be regarded as the same for each, since two bodies cannot occupy the same place, and place is an accident. Wherefore it is because men are plural by their accidents that they are plural in number.

---

[8] The terms differentia, numerus, species, are used expertly, as would be expected of the author of the In Isag. Porph. Commenta. See S. Brandt's edition of that work (in the Vienna Corpus, 1906), s.v. differencia, etc.

[9] This method of mental abstraction is employed more elaborately in Tr. iii. (vide infra, p. 44) and in Cons. v. pr. 4, where the notion of divine foreknowledge is abstracted in imagination.

CHAPTER II.

We will now begin a careful consideration of each several point, as far as they can be grasped and understood; for it has been wisely said, [10] in my opinion, that it is a scholar's duty to study the real nature of anything before he formulates his belief about it.

Speculative Science may he divided into three kinds: [11] Physics, Mathematics, and Theology. Physics deals with motion and is not abstract or separable (i.e.); for it is concerned with the forms of bodies together with their constituent matter, which forms cannot be separated in reality from their bodies. [12] As the bodies are in motion--the earth, for instance, tending downwards, and fire tending upwards, form takes on the movement of the particular thing to which it is annexed.

Mathematics does not deal with motion and is not abstract, for it investigates forms of bodies apart from matter, and therefore apart from movement, which forms, however, being connected with matter cannot be really separated from bodies.

Theology does not deal with motion and is abstract and separable, for time Divine Substance is without either matter or motion. In Physics, then, we are bound to use scientific, in Mathematics, systematical, in Theology, intellectual concepts; and in Theology we will not let ourselves be diverted to play with imaginations, but will simply apprehend that Form which is pure form and no image, which is very Being and the source of Being For everything owes its being to Form. Thus a statue is not a statue on account of the brass which is its matter, but on account of the form whereby the likeness of a living thing is impressed upon it: the brass itself is not brass because of the earth which is its matter, but because of its form. Likewise earth is not earth by reason of unqualified matter, [13] but by reason of dryness and weight, which are forms. So nothing is said to be because it has matter, but because it has a distinctive form. But the Divine Substance is Form without matter, and is therefore One, and is its own essence. But other things are not simply their own essences, for each thing has its being from the things of which it is composed, that is, from its parts. It is This and That, i.e. it is the totality of its parts in conjunction; it is not This or That taken apart. Earthly man, for instance, since he consists of soul and body, is soul and body, not soul or body, separately; therefore

TRINITY IS ONE GOD NOT THREE GODS

he is not his own essence. That on the other hand which does not consist of This and That, but only of This, is really its own essence, and is altogether beautiful and stable because it is not grounded in any alien element. Wherefore that is truly One in which is no number, in which nothing is present except its own essence. Nor can it become the substrate of anything, for it is pure Form, and pure Forms cannot be substrates. [14] For if humanity, like other forms, is a substrate for accidents, it does not receive accidents through the fact that it exists, but through the fact that matter is subjected to it. Humanity appears indeed to appropriate the accident which in reality belongs to the matter underlying the conception Humanity. But Form which, is without matter cannot be a substrate, and cannot have its essence in matter, else it would not be form but a reflexion. For from those forms which are outside matter come the forms which are in matter and produce bodies. We misname the entities that reside in bodies when we call them forms; they are mere images; they only resemble those forms which are not incorporate in matter. In Him, then, is no difference, no plurality arising out of difference, no multiplicity arising out of accidents, and accordingly no number.

[10] By Cicero (Tusc. v. 7. 19).
[11] Cf. the similar division of philosophy in Isag. Porph. ed. Brandt, pp 7 ff.
[12] Sb. Though they may be separated in thought.
[13] of Aristotle. Cf. (Alexander Aphrod. De Anima, 17. 17); (id. De anima libri mantissa, 124. 77).
[14] This is Realism. Cf. "Sed si rerum ueritatem atque integritatem perpendas, non est dubium quin uere sint. Nam cum res omnes quae uere sunt sine his quinque (i.e. genus species differentia propria accidentia) esse non possint, has ipsas quinque res uere intellectas esse non dubites". Isag. In Porph. ed. pr. i. (M. P.L. lxiv. Col. 19, Brandt, pp. 26 ff.). The two passages show that Boethius is definitly commited to the Realistic position, although in his Comment. In Porphyr. A se translatum he holds the scales between Plato and Aristotle, "quorum diiudicare sententias aptum esse non duxi" (cp. Haureau, Hist. De la philosophie scolastique, i. 120). As a fact in the Comment. in Porph. he merely postpones the question, which in the De Trin. he settles, Boethius was ridiculed in the Middle Ages for his caution.

CHAPTER III.

Now God differs from God in no respect for there cannot lie divine essences distinguished either by accidents or by substantial differences belonging to a substrate. But where there is no difference, there is no sort of plurality and accordingly no number; here, therefore, is unity alone. For whereas we say God thrice when we name the Father, Son, and Holy Spirit, these three unities do not produce a plurality of number in their own essences, if we think of what we count instead of what we count with. For in the case of abstract number a repetition of single items does produce plurality; but in the case of concrete number the repetition and plural use of single items does not by any means produce numerical difference in the objects counted. There are as a fact two kinds of number. There is the number with which we count (abstract) and the number inherent in the things counted (concrete). "One" is a thing--the thing counted. Unity is that by which oneness is denoted. Again " two "belongs to the class of things as men or stones; but not so duality; duality is merely that whereby two men or two stones are denoted; and so on. Therefore a repetition of unities [15] produces plurality when it is a question of abstract, but not when it is a question of concrete things, as, for example, if I say of one and the same thing, "one sword, one brand, one blade." [16] It is easy to see that each of these names denotes a sword; I am not numbering unities but simply repeating one thing, and in saying "sword, brand, blade," I reiterate the one thing and do not enumerate several different things any more than I produce three suns instead of merely mentioning one thing thrice when I say "Sun, Sun, Sun."

So then if God be predicated thrice of Father, Sun, and Holy Spirit, the threefold predication does not result in plural number. The risk of that, as has been said, attends only on those who distinguish Them according to merit. But Catholic Christians, allowing no difference of merit in God, assuming Him to be Pure Form and believing Him to he nothing else than His own essence, rightly regard the statement "the Father is God, the Son is God the Holy Spirit is God, and this Trinity is one God," not as an enumeration of different things but as a reiteration of one and the same thing, like the statement, "blade and brand are one sword" or "sun, sun, and sun are one sun."

TRINITY IS ONE GOD NOT THREE GODS

Let this be enough for the present to establish my meaning and to show that not every repetition of units produces number and plurality. Still in saying "Father, Son, and Holy Spirit," we are not using Synonymous terms. "Brand and blade " are the same and identical, but

"Father, Son, and Holy Spirit" though the same, are not identical. This point deserves a moment's consideration. When they ask, "Is the Father the same s the Son ?" Catholics answer "No." "Is the One the same as the Other?" The answer is in the negative. There is not, therefore, complete indifference between Them; and so number does come in--number which we explained was the result of diversity of substrates. We will briefly debate this point when, we have done examining how particular predicates can be applied to God.

[15] e.g. if I say "one, one, one," I enounce three unities.
[16] The same words are used to illustrate the same matter in the Comment. in Arist. 2nd ed. (Meiser) 56. 12.

CHAPTER IV.

There are in all ten categories which can be universally predicated of things, namely, Substance, Quality, Quantity, Relation, Place, Time, Condition, Situation, Activity, Passivity. Their meaning is determined by the contingent subject; for some of them denote real substantive attributes of created things, others belong to the class of accidental attributes. But when these categories are applied to God they change their meaning entirely. Relation, for instance, cannot be predicated at all of God; for substance in Him is not really substantial but super-substantial. So with quality and the other possible attributes, of which we must add examples for the sake of clearness.

When we say God, we seem to denote a substance; but it is a substance that is supersubstantial. When we say of Him, "He is just," we mention a quality, not an accidental quality--rather a substantial and, in fact, a supersubstantial quality. [17] For God is not one thing because He is, and another thing because He is just; with Him to be just and to be God are one and the same. So when we say, "He is great or the greatest, we seem to predicate quantity, but it is a quantity similar to this substance which we have declared to be supersubstantial; for with Him to be great and to be God are all one. Again, concerning His Form, we have already shown that He is Form, and truly One without Plurality. The categories we have mentioned are such that they give to the thing to which they are applied the character which they express; in created things they express divided being, in God, conjoined and united being--in the following manner. When we name a substance, as man or God, it seems as though that of which the predication is made were itself substance, as man or God is substance. But there is a difference: since man is not simply and entirely man, and therefore is not substance after all. For what man is he owes to other things which are not man. But God is simply and entirely God, for He is nothing else than what He is, and therefore is, through simple existence, God. Again we apply just, a quality, as though it were that of which it is predicated; that is, if we say "a just man or just God," we assert that man or God is just. But there is a difference, for man is one thing, and a just man is another thing. But God is justice itself. So a man or God is said to be great, and it would appear that man is substantially great or that God is substantially great. But man is merely great; God is greatness.

TRINITY IS ONE GOD NOT THREE GODS

The remaining categories are not predicable of God nor yet of created things. [18] For place is predicated of man or of God--a man is in the market-place; God is everywhere--but in neither case is the predicate identical with the object of predication. To say "A man is in the market" is quite a different thing from saying "he is white or long," or, so to speak, encompassed and determined by some property which enables him to be described in terms of his substance; this predicate of place simply declares how far his substance is given a particular setting amid other things.

It is otherwise, of course, with God. "He is everywhere" does not mean that He is in every place, for He cannot be in any place at all--but that every place is present to Him for Him to occupy, although He Himself can be received by no place, and therefore He cannot anywhere be in a place, since He is everywhere but in no place. It is the same with the category of time, as, "A man came yesterday; God is ever." Here again the predicate of "coming yesterday" denotes not something substantial, but something happening in terms of time. But the expression "God is ever" denotes a single Present, summing up His continual presence in all the past, in all the present --however that term be used--and in all the future. Philosophers say that "ever" may be applied to the life of the heavens and other immortal bodies. But as applied to God it has a different meaning. He is ever, because "ever" is with Him a term of present time, and there is this great difference between "now," which is our present, and the divine present. Our present connotes changing time and sempiternity; God's present, unmoved, and immoveable, connotes eternity. Add semper to eternity and you get the constant, incessant and thereby perpetual course of our present time, that is to say, sempiternity. [19]

It is just the same with the categories of condition and activity. For example, we say "A man runs, clothed," "God rules, possessing all things." Here again nothing substantial is asserted of either subject; in fact all the categories we have hitherto named arise from what lies outside substance, and all of them, so to speak, refer to something other than substance. The difference between the categories is easily seen by an example. Thus, the terms "man" and "God" refer to the substance in virtue of which the subject is--man or God. The term "just " refers to the quality in virtue of which the subject is something, viz. just; the term "great" to the quantity in virtue of which He is something, viz, great. No other category save substance, quality, and quantity refer to the substance of the subject. If I say of one "he is in the market" or "everywhere," I am applying the category of place, which is not a category of the substance, like "just" in virtue of justice. So if I say, "he runs, He rules, he is now, He is ever," I make reference to activity or time--if indeed God's "ever" can be described as time--but not to a category of substance, like "great" in virtue of greatness.

Finally, we must not look for the categories of situation and passivity in God, for they simply are not to be found in Him.

Have I now made clear the difference between the categories? Some denote the reality of a thing; others its accidental circumstances; the former declare that a thing is something; the latter say nothing about its being anything, but simply attach to it, so to speak, something external. Those categories which describe a thing in terms of its substance may be called substantial categories; when they apply to things as subjects they are called accidents. In reference to God, who is not a subject at all, it is only possible to employ the category of substance.

---

[17] Gilbert de la Porree in his commentary on the De Trin. Makes Boethius's meaning clear. "Quad igitur in illo substantiam nominamus, non est subiectionis ratione quod dicitur, sed ultra omnem quae accidentibus est subiecta substantiam est essentia, absque omnibus quae possunt accidere solitaria omnino" (Migne, P.L. lxiv. 1283). Cf. Aug. De Trin. vii. 10.

[18] i.e. according to their substance.

[19] The doctrine is Augustine's, cf. De Ciu. Dei, xi. 6, xii. 16; but Boethius's use of sempiternitas, as well as his word-building, seem to be peculiar to himself. Claudianus Mamertus, speaking of applying the categories to God, uses sempiternitas as Boethius uses aeternitas. Cf. De Statu Animae i. 19. Apuleius seems to use both terms interchangeably, e.g. Asclep. 29-31. On Boethius's distinction between time and eternity see Cons. v. pr. 6, and Rand, Der dem B. zugeschr. Trakt. De fide, pp. 425 ff, and Brandt in Theol. Littzg., 1902, p. 147.

CHAPTER V.

Let us now consider the category of relation, to which all the foregoing remarks have been preliminary; for qualities which obviously arise from the association of another term do not appear to predicate anything concerning the substance of a subject. For instance, master and slave [20] are relative terms; let us see whether either of them are predicates of substance. If you suppress the term slave, [21] you simultaneously suppress the term master. On the other hand, though you suppress the term whiteness, you do not suppress some white thing, [22] though, of course, if the particular whiteness inhere as an accident in the thing, the thing disappears as soon as you suppress the accidental quality whiteness. But in the case of master, if you suppress the term slave, the term master disappears. But slave is not an accidental quality of master, as whiteness is of a white thing; it denotes the power which the master has over the slave. Now since the power goes when the slave is removed, it is plain that power is no accident to the substance of master, but is an adventitious augmentation arising from the possession of slaves.

It cannot therefore be affirmed that a category of relation increases, decreases, or alters in any way the substance of the thing to which it is applied. The category of relation, then, has nothing to do with the substance of the subject; it simply denotes a condition of relativity, and that not necessarily to something else, but sometimes to the subject itself. For suppose a man standing. If I go up to him on my right and stand beside him, he will be left, in relation to me, not because he is left in himself, but because I have come up to him on my right. Again, if I come up to him on my left, he becomes right in relation to me, not because he is right in himself, as he may be white or long, but because he is right in virtue of my approach. What he is depends entirely on me, and not in the least on the essence of his being.

Accordingly those predicates which do not denote the essential property of a thing cannot alter, change or disturb its nature in any way. Wherefore if Father and Son are predicates of relation, and, as we have said, have no other difference but that of relation, and if relation is not asserted of its subject as though it were time subject itself and its substantial quality, it will effect no real difference in its subject, but, in a phrase which aims at interpreting what we can hardly understand, a difference of persons. For it is a canon of absolute truth that distinctions in incorporeal things are established by differences and not by spatial separation. It cannot be said that God became Father by the addition to His substance of some accident; for he never began to be Father, since the begetting of the Son belongs to His very substance; however, time predicate father, as such, is relative. And if we bear in mind all the propositions made God in the previous discussion, we shall admit that God the Son proceeded from God the Father, and the Holy Ghost from both, and that They cannot possibly be spatially different, since They are incorporeal. But since the Father is God, the Son is God, and the Holy Spirit is God, and since there are in God no points of difference distinguishing Him from God, He differs from none of the Others. But where there are no differences there is no plurality; where is no plurality there is Unity. Again, nothing but God can be begotten of God, and lastly, in concrete enumerations the repetition of units does not produce plurality. Thus the Unity of the Three is suitably established.

[20] Dominus and seruus are similarly used as illustration, In Cat. (Migne, P.L. lxiv. 217).
[21] i.e. which is external to the master.
[22] i.e. which is external to the whitened thing.

CHAPTER VI.

But since no relation can be affirmed of one subject alone, inasmuch as a predicate wanting relation is a predicate of substance, the manifoldness of the category of relation, Trinity is secured through the category of relation, and the Unity is maintained through the fact that there is no difference of substance, or operation, or generally of any substantial predicate. So then, the divine substance preserves the Unity, the divine relations bring about the Trinity. Hence only terms belonging to relation may be applied singly to Each. For the Father is not the same as the Son, nor is either of Them the same as the Holy Spirit. Yet Father, Son, and Holy Spirit are each the same God, the same in justice, in goodness, in greatness, and in everything that can he predicated of substance. One must not forget that predicates of relativity do not always involve relation to something other than the subject, as slave involves master, where the two terms are different. For equals are equal, like are like, identicals are identical, each with other, and the relation of Father to Son, and of both to Holy Spirit is a relation of identicals. A relation of this kind is not to be found in created things, but that is because of the difference which we know attaches to transient objects. We must not in speaking of God let imagination lead us astray; we must let the Faculty of pure Knowledge lift us up and teach us to know all things as far as they may be known. [23]

I have now finished the investigation which I proposed. The exactness of my reasoning awaits the standard of your judgment; your authority will pronounce whether I have seen a straight path to the goal. If, God helping me, I have furnished some support in argument to an article which stands by itself on the firm foundation of Faith, I shall render joyous praise for the finished work to Him from whom the invitation comes. But if human nature has failed to reach beyond its limits, whatever is lost through my infirmity must be made good by my intention.

[23] Cf. Cons. v. pr. 4 and 5, especially in pr. 5 the passage "quare in illius summae intellegentiae acumen si possumus erigamur."
[6] Cf. The discussion of human ratio and divine intellegetia in Cons. v. pr. 4 and 5.
[7] e.g. Aug. De Trin.

CONSOLATION OF PHILOSOPHY

By

ANICIUS MANLIUS SEVERINUS BOETHIUS

BOOK I

To pleasant songs my work was erstwhile given, and bright were all my labours then; but now in tears to sad refrains am I compelled to turn. Thus my maimed Muses guide my pen, and gloomy songs make no feigned tears bedew my face. Then could no fear so overcome to leave me companionless upon my way. They were the pride of my earlier bright-lived days: in my later gloomy days they are the comfort of my fate; for hastened by unhappiness has age come upon me without warning, and grief hath set within me the old age of her gloom. White hairs are scattered untimely on my head, and the skin hangs loosely from my worn-out limbs.

Happy is that death which thrusts not itself upon men in their pleasant years, yet comes to them at the oft-repeated cry of their sorrow. Sad is it how death turns away from the unhappy with so deaf an ear, and will not close, cruel, the eyes that weep. Ill is it to trust to Fortune's fickle bounty, and while yet she smiled upon me, the hour of gloom had well-nigh overwhelmed my head. Now has the cloud put off its alluring face, wherefore without scruple my life drags out its wearying delays.

Why, O my friends, did ye so often puff me up, telling me that I was fortunate? For he that is fallen low did never firmly stand.'

While I was pondering thus in silence, and using my pen to set down so tearful a complaint, there appeared standing over my head a woman's form, whose countenance was full of majesty, whose eyes shone as with fire and in power of insight surpassed the eyes of men, whose colour was full of life, whose strength was yet intact though she was so full of years that none would ever think that she was subject to such age as ours. One could but doubt her varying stature, for at one moment she repressed it to the common measure of a man, at another she seemed to touch with her crown the very heavens: and when she had raised higher her head, it pierced even the sky and baffled the sight of those who would look upon it. Her clothing was wrought of the finest thread by subtle workmanship brought to an indivisible piece. This had she woven with her own hands, as I afterwards did learn by her own shewing. Their beauty was somewhat dimmed by the dulness of long neglect, as is seen in the smoke-grimed masks of our ancestors. On the border below was inwoven the symbol P, on that above was to be read a Th [1] And between the two letters there could be marked degrees, by which, as by the rungs of a ladder, ascent might be made from the lower principle to the higher. Yet the hands of rough men had torn this garment and snatched such morsels as they could therefrom. In her right hand she carried books, in her left was a sceptre brandished.

When she saw that the Muses of poetry were present by my couch giving words to my lamenting, she was stirred a while; her eyes flashed fiercely, and said she, Who has suffered these seducing mummers to approach this sick man? Never do they support those in sorrow by any healing remedies, but rather do ever foster the sorrow by poisonous sweets. These are they who stifle the fruit-bearing harvest of reason with the barren briars of the passions: they free not the minds of men from disease, but accustom them thereto. I would think it less grievous if your allurements drew away from me some uninitiated man, as happens in the vulgar herd. In such an one my labours would be naught harmed, but this man has been nourished in the lore of Eleatics and Academics; and to him have ye reached? Away with you, Sirens, seductive unto destruction! leave him to my Muses to be cared for and to be healed.'

Their band thus rated cast a saddened glance upon the ground, confessing their shame in blushes, and passed forth dismally over the threshold. For my part, my eyes were dimmed with tears, and I could not discern who was this woman of such commanding power. I was amazed, and turning my eyes to the ground I began in silence to await what she should do. Then she approached nearer and sat down upon the end of my couch: she looked into my face heavy with grief and cast down by sorrow to the ground, and then she raised her complaint over the trouble of my mind in these words.

Ah me! how blunted grows the mind when sunk below the o'erwhelming flood! Its own true light no longer burns within, and it would break forth to outer dark nesses. How often care, when fanned by earthly winds, grows to a larger and unmeasured bane. This man has been free to the open heaven: his habit has it been to wander into the paths of the sky: his to watch the light of the bright sun, his to inquire into the brightness of the chilly moon; he, like a conqueror, held fast bound in its order every star that makes its wandering circle, turning its peculiar course. Nay, more, deeply has he searched into the springs of nature, whence came the roaring blasts that ruffle the ocean's bosom calm: what is the spirit that makes the firmament revolve; wherefore does the evening star sink into the western wave but to rise from the radiant East; what is the cause which so tempers the season of Spring that it decks the earth with rose-blossoms; whence comes it to pass that Autumn is prolific in the years of plenty and overflows with teeming vines: deeply to search these causes was his wont, and to bring forth secrets deep in Nature hid.

Now he lies there; extinct his reason's light, his neck in heavy chains thrust down, his countenance with grievous weight downcast; ah! the brute earth is all he can behold.

But now,' said she, is the time for the physician's art, rather than for complaining.' Then fixing her eyes wholly on me, she said, Are you the man who was nourished upon the milk of my learning, brought up with my food until you had won you r way to the power of a manly soul? Surely I had given you such weapons as would keep you safe, and your strength unconquered; if you had not thrown them away. Do you know me? Why do you keep silence? Are you dumb from shame or from dull amazement? I would it were from shame, but I see that amazement has overwhelmed you.'

When she saw that I was not only silent, but utterly tongue-tied and dumb, she put her hand gently upon my breast, and said, There is no danger: he is suffering from drowsiness, that disease which attacks so many minds which have been deceived. He has forgotten himself for a moment and will quickly remember, as soon as he recognises me. That he may do so, l et me brush away from his eyes the darkening cloud of thoughts of matters perishable.' So saying, she gathered her robe into a fold and dried my swimming eyes.

Then was dark night dispelled, the shadows fled away, and my eyes received returning power as before. 'Twas just as when the heavenly bodies are enveloped by the west wind's rush, and the sky stands thick with watery clouds; the sun is hidden and the stars are not yet come into the sky, and night descending from above o'erspreads the earth: but if the north wind smites this scene, launched forth from the Thracian cave, it unlocks the imprisoned daylight; the sun shines forth, and thus sparkling Phoebus smites with his rays our wondering eyes.

CONSOLATION OF PHILOSOPHY

In such a manner were the clouds of grief scattered. Then I drew breath again and engaged my mind in taking knowledge of my physician's countenance. So when I turned my eyes towards her and fixed my gaze upon her, I recognised my nurse, Philosophy, in whose chambers I had spent my life from earliest manhood. And I asked her, Wherefore have you, mistress of all virtues, come down from heaven above to visit my lonely place of banishment? Is it that you, as well as I, may be harried, the victim of false charges?' Should I,' said she, desert you, my nursling? Should I not share and bear my part of the burden which has been laid upon you from spite against my name? Surely Philosophy never allowed herself to let the innocent go upon their journey unbefriended. Think you I would fear calumnies? that I would be terrified as though they were a new misfortune? Think you that this is the first time that wisdom has been harassed by d angers among men of shameless ways? In ancient days before the time of my child, Plato, have we not as well as nowadays fought many a mighty battle against the recklessness of folly? And though Plato did survive, did not his master, Socrates, win hi s victory of an unjust death, with me present at his side? When after him the followers of Epicurus, and in turn the Stoics, and then others did all try their utmost to seize his legacy, they dragged me, for all my cries and struggles, as though to s hare me as plunder; they tore my robe which I had woven with mine own hands, and snatched away the fragments thereof: and when they thought I had altogether yielded myself to them, they departed. And since among them were to be seen certain signs of my outward bearing, others ill-advised did think they wore my livery: thus were many of them undone by the errors of the herd of uninitiated. But if you have not heard of the exile of Anaxagoras, [2] nor the poison drunk by Socrates, [3] nor the torture of Zeno, [4] which all were of foreign lands, yet you may know of Canius, [5] Seneca, [6] and Soranus, [7] whose fame is neither small nor passing old. Naught else brought them to ruin but that, being built up in my ways, they appeared at variance with the desires of unscrupulous men. So it is no matter for your wonder if, in this sea of life, we are tossed about by storms from all sides; for to oppose evil men is the chief aim we set before ourselves. Though the band of such men is great in numbers, yet is it to be contemned: for it is guided by no leader, but is hurried along at random only by error running riot everywhere. If this band when warring against us presses too strongly upon us, our leader, Reason, gathers her forces into her citadel, while the enemy are busied in plundering useless baggage. As they seize the most worthless things, we laugh at them from above, untroubled by the whole band of mad marauders, and we are defended by that rampart to which riotous folly may not hope to attain.

He who has calmly reconciled his life to fate, and set proud death beneath his feet, can look fortune in the face, unbending both to good and bad: his countenance unconquered he can shew. The rage and threatenings of the sea will not move him though they stir from its depths the upheaving swell: Vesuvius's furnaces may never so often burst forth, and he may send rolling upwards smoke and fire; the lightning, whose wont it is to smite down lofty towers, may flash upon its way, but such men shall they never move. Why then stand they wretched and aghast when fierce tyrants rage in impotence? Fear naught, and hope naught: thus shall you have a weak man's rage disarmed. But whoso fears with trembling, or desires aught from them, he stands not firmly rooted, but dependent: thus has he thrown away his shield; he can be rooted up, and he links for himself the very chain whereby he may be dragged.

Are such your experiences, and do they sink into your soul?' she asked. Do you listen only as "the dull ass to the lyre"? Why do you weep? Wherefore flow your tears? "Speak, nor keep secret in thine heart." If you expect a physician to help you, you must lay bare your wound.' Then did I rally my spirit till it was strong again, and answered, Does the savage bitterness of my fortune still need recounting? Does it not stand forth plainly enough of itself? Does not the very aspect of this place strike you? Is this the library which you had chosen for yourself as your sure resting-place in my house? Is this the room in which you would so often tarry with me expounding the philosophy of things human and divine? Was my condition like this, or my countenance, when I probed with your aid the secrets of nature, when you marked out with a wand the courses of the stars, when you shaped our habits and the rule of all our life by the pattern of the universe? [8] Are these the rewards we reap by yielding ourselves to you? Nay, you yourself have established this saying by the mouth of Plato, that commonwealths would be blessed if they were guided by those who made wisdom their study, or if those who guided them would make wisdom their study. [9] By the mouth of that same great man did you teach that this was the binding reason why a commonwealth should be governed by philosophers, namely that the helm of government should not be left to unscrupulous or criminal citizens lest they should bring corruption and ruin upon the good citizens. [10] Since, then, I had learned from you in quiet and inaction of this view, I followed it further, for I desired to practise it in public government. You and God Himself, who has grafted you in the minds of philosophers, are my witnesses that never have I applied myself to any office of state except that I might work for the common welfare of all good men. Thence followed bitter quarrels with evil men which could not be appeased, and, for the sake of preserving justice, contempt of the enmity of those in power, for this is the result of a free and fearless conscience. How often have I withstood Conigastus to his face, whenever he has attacked a weak man's fortune! How often have I turned by force Trigulla, [11] the overseer of the Emperor's household, from an unjust act that he had begun or even carried out! How many times have I put my own authority in danger by protecting those wretched people who were harried with unending false charges by the greed of barbarian Goths which ever went unpunished! Never, I say, has any man depraved me from justice to injustice. My heart has ached as bitterly as those of the sufferers when I have seen the fortunes of our subjects ruined both by the rapacity of persons and the taxes of the state. Again, in a time of severe famine, a grievous, intolerable sale by compulsion was decreed in Campania, and devastation threatened that province. Then I undertook for the sake of the common welfare a struggle against the commander of the Imperial guard; though the king was aware of it, I fought against the enforcement of the sale, and fought successfully. Paulinus was a man who had been consul: the jackals of the court had in their own hopes and desires already swallowed up his possessions, but I snatched him from their very gaping jaws. I exposed myself to the hatred of the treacherous informer Cyprian, that I might prevent Albinus, also a former consul, being overwhelmed by the penalty of a trumped-up charge. Think you that I have raised up against myself bitter and great quarrels enough? But I ought to have been safer among those whom I helped; for, from my love of justice, I laid up for myself among the courtiers no resource to which I might turn for safety. Who, further, were the informers upon whose evidence I was banished? One was Basilius: he was formerly expelled from the royal service, and was driven by debt to inform against me. Again, Opilio and Gaudentius had been condemned to exile by the king for many unjust acts and crimes: this decree they would not obey, and they sought sanctuary in sacred buildings, but when the king was aware of it, he declared that if they departed not from Ravenna before a certain day, they should be driven forth branded upon their foreheads. What could be more stringent than this? Yet upon that very day information against me was laid by these same men and accepted. Why so? Did my character deserve this treatment? Or did my prearranged condemnation give credit and justification to my accusers? Did Fortune feel no shame for this? If not for innocence calumniated, at any rate for the baseness of the calumniators?

Would you learn the sum of the charges against me? It was said that "I had desired the safety of the Senate." You would learn in what way. I was charged with "having hindered an informer from producing papers by which the Senate could be accused of treason." What think you, my mistress? Shall I deny it lest it shame you? Nay, I did desire the safety of the Senate, nor shall ever cease to desire it. Shall I confess it? Then there would have been no need to hinder an informer. Shall I call it a crime to have wished for the safety of that order? By its own decrees concerning myself it has established that this is a crime. Though want of foresight often deceives itself, it cannot alter the merits of facts, and, in obedience to the Senate's command, I cannot think it right to hide the truth or to assent to falsehood.

However, I leave it to your judgment and that of philosophers to decide how the justice of this may be; but I have committed to writing for history the true course of events, that posterity may not be ignorant thereof. I think it unnecessary to speak of the forged letters through which I am accused of " hoping for the freedom of Rome." Their falsity would have been apparent if I had been free to question the evidence of the informers themselves, for their confessions have much force in all such business.

But what avails it? No liberty is left to hope for. Would there were any! I would answer in the words of Canius, who was accused by Gaius Cæsar, [12] Germanicus's son, of being cognisant of a plot against himself: " If I had known of it, you would not have."

And in this matter grief has not so blunted my powers that I should complain of wicked men making impious attacks upon virtue: but at this I do wonder, that they should hope to succeed. Evil desires are, it may be, due to our natural failings, but that the conceptions of any wicked mind should prevail against innocence while God watches over us, seems to me unnatural. Wherefore not without cause has one of your own followers asked, " If Go d is, whence come evil things? If He is not, whence come good? "

Again, let impious men, who thirst for the blood of the whole Senate and of all good citizens, be allowed to wish for the ruin of us too whom they recognise as champions of the Senate and all good citizens: but surely such as I have not deserved the same hatred from the members of the Senate too?

Since you were always present to guide me in my words and my deeds, I think you re member what happened at Verona. When King Theodoric, desiring the common ruin of the Senate, was for extending to the whole order the charge of treason laid against Albinus, you remember how I laboured to defend the innocence of the order without any care for my own danger? You know that I declare this truthfully and with no boasting praise of self. For the secret value of a conscience, that approves its own action, is lessened somewhat each time that it receives the reward of fame by displaying its deeds. But you see what end has fallen upon my innocency. In the place of the rewards of honest virtue, I am suffering the punishments of an ill deed that was not mine. And did ever any direct confession of a crime find its judges so well agreed upon exercising harshness, that neither the liability of the human heart to err, nor the changeableness of the fortune of all mankind, could yield one dissentient voice? If it had been said that I had wished to burn down temples, to murder with sacrilegious sword their priests, that I had planned the massacre of all good citizens, even so I should have been present to plead guilty or to be convicted, before the sentence was executed. But here am I, nearly five hundred-miles away, without the opportunity of defending myself, condemned to death and the confiscation of my property because of my too great zeal for the Senate. Ah! well have they deserved that none should ever be liable to be convicted on such a charge! Even those who laid information have seen the honour of this accusation, for, that they might blacken it with some criminal ingredient, they had need to lie, saying that I had violated my conscience by using unholy means to obtain offices corruptly. But you, by being planted within me, dispelled from the chamber of my soul all craving for that which perishes, and where your eyes were looking there could be no place for any such sacrilege. For you instilled into my ears, and thus into my daily thoughts, that saying of Pythagoras, "Follow after God." Nor was it seemly that I, whom you had built up to such excellence that you made me as a god, should seek the support of the basest wills of men. Yet, further, the innocent life within my home, my gathering of most honourable friends, my father-in-law Symmachus, [13] a man esteemed no less in his public life than for his private conscientiousness, these all put far from me all suspicion of this crime. But -- O the shame of it! -- it is from you that they think they derive the warrant for such a charge, and we seem to them to be allied to ill-doing from this very fact that we are steeped in the principles of your teaching, and trained in your manners of life. Thus it is not enough that my deep respect for you has profited me nothing, but you yourself have received wanton contumely from the hatred that had rather fallen on me. Yet besides this, is another load added to my heap of woes: the judgment of the world looks not to the deserts of the case, but to the evolution of chance, and holds that only this has been intended which good fortune may chance to foster: whence it comes that the good opinion of the world is the first to desert the unfortunate. It is wearisome to recall what were the tales by people told, or how little their many various opinions agreed. This alone I would fain say: it is the last burden laid upon us by unkind fortune, that when any charge is invented to be fastened upon unhappy men, they are believed to have deserved all they have to bear. For kindness I have received persecutions; I have been driven from all my possessions, stripped of my honours, and stained for ever in my reputation. I think I see the intoxication of joy in the sin-steeped dens of criminals: I see the most abandoned of men intent upon new and evil schemes of spying: I see honest men lying crushed with the fear which smites them after the result of my perilous case: wicked men one and all encouraged to dare every crime without fear of punishment, nay, with hope of rewards for the accomplishment thereof: the innocent I see robbed not merely of their peace and safety, but even of all chance of defending themselves. So then I may cry aloud: --

Founder of the star-studded universe, resting on Thine eternal throne whence Thou turnest the swiftly rolling sky, and bindest the stars to keep Thy law; at Thy word the moon now shines brightly with full face, ever turned to her brother's light, and so she dims the lesser lights; or now she is herself obscured, for nearer to the sun her beams shew her pale horns alone. Cool rises the evening star at night's first drawing nigh: the same is the morning star who casts off the harness that she bore before, and paling meets the rising sun. When winter's cold doth strip the trees, Thou settest a shorter span to day. And Thou, when summer comes to warm, dost change the short divisions of the night. Thy power doth order the seasons of the year, so that the western breeze of spring brings back the leaves which winter's north wind tore away; so that the dog-star's heat makes ripe the ears of corn whose seed Arcturus watched. Naught breaks that ancient law: naught leaves undone the work appointed to its place. Thus all things Thou dost rule with limits fixed: the lives of men alone dost Thou scorn to restrain, as a guardian, within bounds. For why does Fortune with her fickle hand deal out such changing lots? The hurtful penalty is due to crime, but falls upon the sinless head: depraved men rest at ease on thrones aloft, and by their unjust lot can spurn beneath their hurtful heel the necks of virtuous men. Beneath obscuring shadows lies bright virtue hid: the just man bears the unjust's infamy. They suffer not for forsworn oaths, they suffer not for crimes glozed over with their lies. But when their will is to put forth their strength, with triumph they subdue the mightiest kings whom peoples in their thousands fear. O Thou who dost weave the bonds of Nature's self, look down upon this pitiable earth! Mankind is no base part of this great work, and we are tossed on Fortune's wave. Rest rain, our Guardian, the engulfing surge, and as Thou dost the unbounded heaven rule, with a like bond make true and firm these lands.'

While I grieved thus in long-drawn pratings, Philosophy looked on with a calm countenance, not one whit moved by my complaints Then said she, When I saw you in grief and in tears I knew thereby that you were unhappy and in exile, but I knew not how distant was your exile until your speech declare d it. But you have not been driven so far from your home; you have wandered thence yourself: or if you would rather hold that you have been driven, you have been driven by yourself rather than by any other. No other could have done so to you. For if you recall your true native country, you know that it is not under the rule of the many-headed people, as was Athens of old, but there is one Lord, one King, who rejoices in the greater number of his subjects, not in their banishment. To be guided by his reins, to bow to his justice, is the highest liberty. Know you not that sacred and ancient law of your own state by which it is enacted that no man, who would establish a dwelling-place for himself therein, may lawfully be put forth? For there is no fear that any man should merit exile, if he be kept safe therein by its protecting walls. But any man that may no longer wish to dwell there, does equally no longer deserve to be there. Wherefore it is your looks rather than the aspect of this place which disturb me. [14] It is not the walls of your library, decked with ivory and glass, that I need, but rather the resting-place in your heart, wherein I have not stored books, but I have of old put that which gives value to books, a store of thoughts from books of mine. As to your services to the common weal, you have spoken truly, though but scantily, if you consider your manifold exertions. Of all wherewith you have been charged either truthfully or falsely, you have but recorded what is well known. As for the crimes and wicked lies of the informers, you have rightly thought fit to touch but shortly thereon, for they are better and more fruitfully made common in the mouth of the crowd that discusses all matters. You have loudly and strongly upbraided the unjust ingratitude of the Senate: you have grieved over the charges made against myself, and shed tears over the insult to my fair fame: your last outburst of wrath was against Fortune, when you complained that she paid no fair rewards according to deserts: finally, you have prayed with passionate Muse that the same peace and order, that are seen in the heavens, might also rule the earth. But you are overwhelmed by this variety of mutinous passions: grief, rage, and gloom tear your mind asunder, and so in this present mood stronger measures cannot yet come nigh to heal you. Let us therefore use gentler means, and since, just as matter in the body hardens into a swelling, so have these disquieting influences, let these means soften by kindly handling the unhealthy spot, until it will bear a sharper remedy.

When the sign of the crab doth scorch the field, fraught with the sun's most grievous rays, the husbandman that has freely intrusted his seed to the fruitless furrow, is cheated by the faithless harvest-goddess; and he must turn him to the oak tree's fruit.

When the field is scarred by the bleak north winds, wouldst thou seek the wood's dark carpet to gather violets? If thou wilt enjoy the grapes, wouldst thou seek with clutching hand to prune the vines in spring? 'Tis in autumn Bacchus brings his gifts. Thus God marks out the times and fits to them peculiar works: He has set out a course of change, and lets no confusion come. If aught betake itself to headlong ways, and leaves its sure design, ill will the outcome be thereto.

First then,' she continued, will you let me find out and make trial of the state of your mind by a few small questions, that so I may understand what should be the method of your treatment?'

Ask,' said I, what your judgment would have you ask, and I will answer you.'

Then said she, 'Think you that this universe is guided only at random and by mere chance? or think you there is any rule of reason constituted in it?'

'No, never would I think it could be so, nor believe that such sure motions could be made at random or by chance. I know that God, the founder of the universe, does overlook His work; nor ever may that day come which shall drive me to abandon this belief as untrue.'

'So is it,' she said, 'and even so you cried just now, and only mourned that mankind alone has no part in this divine guardianship: you were fixed in your belief that all other things are ruled by reason. Yet, how strange! how much I wonder how it is that you can be so sick though you are set in such a health-giving state of mind! But let us look deeper into it: I cannot but think there is something lacking. Since you are not in doubt that the universe is ruled by God, tell me by what method you think that government is guided?'

'I scarcely know the meaning of your question; much less can I answer it.'

'Was I wrong,' said she, 'to think that something was lacking, that there was some opening in your armour, some way by which this distracting disease has crept into your soul? But tell me, do you remember what is the aim and end of all things? what the object to which all nature tends?'

'I have heard indeed, but grief has blunted my memory.'

'But do you not some how know whence all things have their source?'

'Yes,' I said; 'that source is God.'

'Is it possible that you, who know the beginning of all things, should not know their end? But such are the ways of these distractions, such is their power, that though they can move a man's position, they cannot pluck him from himself or wrench him from his roots. But this question would I have you answer: do you remember that you are a man?'

BOETHIUS

How can I but remember that?'

Can you then say what is a man?'

Need you ask? I know that he is an animal, reasoning and mortal; that I know, and that I confess myself to be.'

Know you naught else that you are?' asked Philosophy.

Naught,' said I.

Now,' said she, I know the cause, or the chief cause, of your sickness. You have forgotten what you are. Now therefore I have found out to the full the manner of your sickness, and how to attempt the restoring of your health. You are overwhelmed by this forgetfulness of yourself: hence you have been thus sorrowing that you are exiled and robbed of all your possessions. You do not know the aim and end of all things; hence you think that if men are worthless and wicked, they are powerful and fortunate. You have forgotten by what methods the universe is guided; hence you think that the chances of good and bad fortune are tossed about with no ruling hand. These things may lead not to disease only, but even to death as well. But let us thank the Giver of all health, that your nature has not altogether left you. We have yet the chief spark for your health's fire, for you have a true knowledge of the hand that guides the universe: you do believe that its government is not subject to random chance, but to divine reason. Therefore have no fear. From this tiny spark the fire of life shall forthwith shine upon you. But it is not time to use severer remedies, and since we know that it is the way of all minds to clothe themselves ever in false opinions as they throw off the true, and these false ones breed a dark distraction which confuses the true insight, therefore will I try to lessen this darkness for a while with gentle applications of easy remedies, that so the shadows of deceiving passions may be dissipated, and you may have power to perceive the brightness of true light.'

When the stars are hidden by black clouds, no light can they afford. When the boisterous south wind rolls along the sea and stirs the surge, the water, but now as clear as glass, bright as the fair sun's light, is dark, impenetrable to sight, with stirred and scattered sand. The stream, that wanders down the mountain's side, must often find a stumbling-block, a stone within its path torn from the hill's own rock. So too shalt thou: if thou wouldst see the truth in undimmed light, choose the straight road, the beaten path; away with passing joys! away with fear! put vain hopes to flight! and grant no place to grief! Where these distractions reign, the mind is clouded o'er, the soul is bound in chains.'

[1] P and Th are the first letters of the Greek words denoting Practical and Theoretical, the two divisions of philosophy.
[2] Anaxagoras went into exile from Athens about 450 B.C.
[3] Socrates was executed by the Athenian state, B.C. 399.
[4] Zeno of Elea was tortured by Nearchus, tyrant of Elea, about 440 B.C.
[5] Canius was put to death by Caligula, c. A.D. 40.
[6] Seneca was driven to commit suicide by Nero, A.D. 66.
[7] Soranus was condemned to death by Nero, A.D. 66.
[8] Boethius means that his chief philosophical' studies had been physics, astronomy, and ethics.
[9] Plato, Repub. v. 473.
[10] Plato, Repub. vi. 488, 489.
[11] Conigastus and Trigulla were favourite officers of the Emperor, Theodoric, the Goth: they used their influence with him for the oppression of the weak.
[12] The Emperor Caligula.
[13] Symmachus was executed by Theodoric at the same time as Boethius.
[14] Cp. Prose iv. of this book, p. 9.

BOOK II

THEN for a while she held her peace. But when her silence, so discreet, made my thoughts to cease from straying, she thus began to speak: If I have thoroughly learned the causes and the manner of your sickness, your former good fortune has so affected you that you are being consumed by longing for it. The change of one of her this alone has overturned your peace of mind through your own imagination. I understand the varied disguises of that unnatural state. I know how Fortune is ever most friendly and alluring to those whom she strives to deceive, until she overwhelms them with grief beyond bearing, by deserting them when least expected. If you recall her nature, her ways, or her deserts, you will see that you never had in her, nor have lost with her, aught that was lovely. Yet, I think, I shall not need great labour to recall this to your memory. For then too, when she was at your side with all her flattery, you were wont to reproach her in strong and manly terms; and to revile her with the opinions that you had gathered in worship of me with my favoured ones. But no sudden change of outward affairs can ever come without some upheaval in the mind. Thus has it followed that you, like others, have fallen somewhat away from your calm peace of mind. But it is time now for you to make trial of some gentle and pleasant draught, which by reaching your inmost parts shall prepare the way for yet stronger healing draughts. Try therefore the assuring influence of gentle argument which keeps its straight path only when it holds fast to my instructions. And with this art of orators let my handmaid, the art of song, lend her aid in chanting light or weighty harmonies as we desire.

What is it, mortal man, that has cast you down into grief and mourning? You have seen something unwonted, it would seem, something strange to you. But if you think that Fortune has changed towards you, you are wrong. These are ever her ways: this is her very nature. She has with you preserved her own constancy by her very change. She was ever changeable at the time when she smiled upon you, when she was mocking you with the allurements of false good fortune. You have discovered both the different faces of the blind goddess. To the eyes of others she is veiled in part: to you she has made herself wholly known. If you find her welcome, make use of her ways, and so make no complaining. If she fills you with horror by her treachery, treat her with despite; thrust her away from you, for she tempts you to your ruin. For though she is the cause of this great trouble for you, she ought to have been the subject of calmness and peace. For no man can ever make himself sure that she will never desert him, and thus has she deserted you. Do you reckon such happiness to be prized, which is sure to pass away? Is good fortune dear to you, which is with you for a time and is not sure to stay, and which is sure to bring you unhappiness when it is gone? But seeing that it cannot be stayed at will, and that when it flees away it leaves misery behind, what is such a fleeting thing but a sign of coming misery? Nor should it ever satisfy any man to look only at that which is placed before his eyes. Prudence takes measure of the results to come from all things. The very changeableness of good and bad makes Fortune's threats no more fearful, nor her smiles to be desired. And lastly, when you have once put your neck beneath the yoke of For tune, you must with steadfast heart bear whatever comes to pass within her realm. But if you would dictate the law by which she whom you have freely chosen to be your mistress must stay or go, surely you will be acting without justification; and your very impatience will make more bitter a lot which you cannot change. If you set your sails before the wind, will you not move forward whither the wind drives you, not whither your will may choose to go? If you intrust your seed to the furrow, will you not weigh the rich years and the barren against each other? You have given yourself over to Fortune's rule, and you must bow yourself to your mistress's ways. Are you trying to stay the force of her turning wheel? Ah! dull-witted mortal, if Fortune begin to stay still, she is no longer Fortune.

As thus she turns her wheel of chance with haughty hand, and presses on like the surge of Euripus's tides, fortune now tramples fiercely on a fearsome king, and now deceives no less a conquered man by raising from the ground his humbled face. She hears no wretch's cry, she heeds no tears, but wantonly she mocks the sorrow which her cruelty has made. This is her sport: thus she proves her power; if in the selfsame hour one man is raised to happiness, and cast down in despair, 'tis thus she shews her might.

Now would I argue with you by these few words which Fortune herself might use: and do you consider whether her demands are fair "Why, O man," she might say, "do you daily accuse me with your complainings? What injustice have I wrought upon you? Of what good things have I robbed you? Choose your judge whom you will, and before him strive with me for the right to hold your wealth and honours.

BOETHIUS

If you can prove that any one of these does truly belong to any mortal man, readily will I grant that these you seek to regain were yours. When nature brought you forth from your mother's womb, I received you in my arms naked and bare of all things; I cherished you with my gifts, and I brought you up all too kindly with my favouring care, wherefore now you cannot bear with me, and I surrounded you with glory and all the abundance that was mine to give. Now it pleases me to withdraw my hand: be thankful, as though you had lived upon my loans. You have no just cause of complaint, as though you had really lost what was once your own. Why do you rail against me? I have wrought no violence towards you. Wealth, honours, and all such are within my rights. They are my handmaids; they know their mistress; they come with me and go when I depart. Boldly will I say that if these, of whose loss you com plain, were ever yours, you would never have lost them at all. Am I alone to be stayed from using my rightful power? The heavens may grant bright sunlit days, and hide the same beneath the shade of night. The year may deck the earth's countenance with flowers and fruits, and again wrap it with chilling clouds. The sea may charm with its smoothed surface, but no less justly it may soon bristle in storms with rough waves. Is the insatiate discontent of man to bind me to a constancy which belongs not to my ways? Herein lies my very strength; this is my unchanging sport. I turn my wheel that spins its circle fairly; I delight to make the lowest turn to the top, the highest to the bottom. Come you to the top if you will, but on this condition, that you think it no unfairness to sink when the rule of my game demands it. Do you not know my ways? Have you not heard how Croesus, [15] king of Lydia, who filled even Cyrus with fear but a little earlier, was miserably put upon a pyre of burning faggots, but was saved by rain sent down from heaven? Have you forgotten how Paulus shed tears of respect for the miseries of his captive, King Perses? [16] For what else is the crying and the weeping in tragedies but for the happiness of kings overturned by the random blow of fortune? Have you never learnt in your youth the ancient allegory that in the threshold of Jove's hall there stand two vessels, one full of evil, and one of good? What if you have received more richly of the good? What if I have not ever withheld myself from you? What if my changing nature is itself a reason that you should hope for better things? In any way, let not your spirit eat itself away: you are set in the sphere that is common to all, let your desire therefore be to live with your own lot of life, a subject of the kingdom of the world.

CONSOLATION OF PHILOSOPHY

"If Plenty with o'erflowing horn scatter her wealth abroad, abundantly, as in the storm-tossed sea the sand is cast around, or so beyond all measure as the stars shine forth upon the studded sky in cloudless nights; though she never stay her hand, yet will the race of men still weep and wail. Though God accept their prayers freely and give gold with ungrudging hand, and deck with honours those who deserve them, yet when they are gotten, these gifts seem naught. Wild greed swallows what it has sought, and still gapes wide for more. What bit or bridle will hold within its course this headlong lust, when, whetted by abundance of rich gifts, the thirst for possession burns? Never call we that man rich who is ever trembling in haste and groaning for that he thinks he lack

If Fortune should thus defend herself to you,' said Philosophy, you would have naught, I think, to utter on the other part. But if you have any just defence for your complaining, you must put it forward. We will grant you the opportunity of speaking.'

Then I answered, Those arguments have a fair form and are clothed with all the sweetness of speech and of song. When a man listens to them, they delight him; but only so long. The wretched have a deeper feeling of their misfortunes. Wherefore when these pleasing sounds fall no longer upon the ear, this deep-rooted misery again weighs down the spirit.'

It is so,' she said. For these are not the remedies for your sickness, but in some sort are the applications for your grief which chafes against its cure. When the time comes, I will apply those which are to penetrate deeply. But that you may not be content to think yourself wretched, remember how many and how great have been the occasions of your good fortune. I will not describe how, when you lost your father, men of the highest rank received you into their care: how you were chosen by the chief men in the state to be allied to them by marriage; [17] and you were dear to them before you were ever closely related; which is the most valuable of all relationships. Who hesitated to pronounce you most fortunate for the greatness of your wives' families, for their virtues, and for your blessings in your sons too? I need not speak of those things that are familiar, so I pass over the honours which are denied to most old men, but were granted to you when yet young. I choose to come to the unrivalled crown of your good fortune. If the enjoyment of anything mortal can weigh at all in the balance of good fortune, can your memory of one great day ever be extinguished by any mass of accumulated ills? I mean that day when you saw your two sons proceed forth from your house as consuls together, amid the crowding senators, the eager and applauding populace: when they sat down in the seats of honour and you delivered the speech of congratulation to the king, gaining thereby glory for your talent and your eloquence: when in the circus you sat in the place of honour between the consuls, and by a display of lavishness worthy of a triumphing general, you pleased to the full the multitude who were crowded around in expectation.

While Fortune then favoured you, it seems you flaunted her, though she cherished you as her own darling. You carried off a bounty which she had never granted to any citizen before. Will you then balance accounts with Fortune? This is the first time that she has looked upon you with a grudging eye. If you think of your happy and unhappy circumstances both in number and in kind, you will not be able to say that you have not been fortunate until now. And if you think that you were not fortunate because these things have passed away which then seemed to bring happiness, these things too are passing away, which you now hold to be miserable, wherefore you cannot think that you are wretched now. Is this your first entrance upon the stage of life? Are you come here unprepared and a stranger to the scene? Think you that there is any certainty in the affairs of mankind, when you know that often one swift hour can utterly destroy a man? For though the chances of life may seldom be depended upon, yet the last day of a lifetime seems to be the end of Fortune's power, though it perhaps would stay. What, think you, should we therefore say; that you desert her by dying, or that she deserts you by leaving you?'

When o'er the heaven Phoebus from his rose-red car begins to shed his light abroad, his flames oppress the paling stars and blunt their whitened rays. When the grove grows bright in spring with roses neath the west wind's warming breath, let but the cloudy gale once wildly blow, and their beauty is gone, the thorns alone remain. Often the sea is calmly glistening bright with all untroubled waves, but as often does the north wind stir them up, making the troubling tempest boil. If then the earth's own covering so seldom constant stays, if its changes are so great, shalt thou trust the brittle fortunes of mankind, have faith in fleeting good? For this is sure, and this is fixed by everlasting law, that naught which is brought to birth shall constant here abide.'

CONSOLATION OF PHILOSOPHY

Then I answered her, Cherisher of all the virtues, you tell me but the truth: I cannot deny my rapid successes and my prosperity. But it is such remembrances that torment me more than others. For of all suffering from Fortune, the unhappiest misfortune is to have known a happy fortune.'

But,' said Philosophy, you are paying him penalty for your mistaken expectations, and with this you cannot justly charge your life's circumstances. If you are affected by this empty name of Fortune's gift of happiness, you must listen while I recall how many and how great are your sources of happiness: and thus, if you have possessed that which is the most precious among all Fortune's gifts, and if that is still safe and unharmed in your possession, you will never, while you keep these better gifts, be able to justly charge Fortune with unkindness. Firstly, your wife's father, Symmachus, is still living and hale; and what more precious glory has the human race than him? And he, because your worth is undiminished and your life still so valuable, is mourning for the injustice you suffer, this man who is wholly made up of wisdom and virtue. Again, your wife lives, a woman whose character is full of virtue, whose modesty excels its kind; a woman who (to put in a word the gifts she brought you) is like her father. She lives, and, hating this life, for your sake alone she clings to it. Herein only will I yield to allow you unhappiness; she pines with tears and grief through her longing for you. Need I speak of your sons who have both been consuls, and whose lives, as when they were boys, are yet bright with the character of their grandfather and their father? Wherefore, since mortals desire exceedingly to keep a hold on life, how happy you should be, knew you but your blessings, since you have still what none doubts to be dearer than life itself? Wherefore now dry your tears. Fortune's hatred has not yet been so great as to destroy all your holds upon happiness: the tempest that is fallen upon you is not too great for you: your anchors hold yet firm, and they should keep ever nigh to you confidence in the present and hope for future time.

And may they continue to hold fast,' said I, that is my prayer: while they are firm, we will reach the end of our voyage, however things may be. But you see how much my glory has departed.'

And she answered, We have made some progress, if you are not now weary entirely of your present lot. But I cannot bear this dallying so softly, so long as you complain that your happiness lacks aught, so long as you are full of sorrow and care. Whose happiness is so firmly established that he has no quarrel from any side with his estate of life? For the condition of our welfare is a matter fraught with care: either its completeness never appears, or it never remains. One man's wealth is abundant, but his birth and breeding put him to shame. Another is famous for his noble birth, but would rather be unknown because he is hampered by his narrow means. A third is blessed with wealth and breeding, but bewails his life because he has no wife. Another is happy in his marriage, but has no children, and saves his wealth only for an heir that is no son of his. Another is blessed with children, but weeps tears of sorrow for the misdeeds of son or daughter. So none is readily at peace with the lot his fortune sends him. For in each case there is that which is unknown to him who has not experienced it, and which brings horror to him who has experienced it. Consider further, that the feelings of the most fortunate men are the most easily affected, wherefore, unless all their desires are supplied, such men, being unused to all adversity, are cast down by every little care: so small are the troubles which can rob them of complete happiness.

How many are they, think you, who would think themselves raised to heaven if the smallest part of the remnants of your good fortune fell to them? This very place, which you call a place of exile, is home to those who live herein. Thus there is nothing wretched unless you think it to be so: and in like manner he who bears all with a calm mind finds his lot wholly blessed. Who is so happy but would wish to change his estate, if he yields to impatience of his lot? With how much bitterness is the sweetness of man's life mingled! For even though its enjoyment seem pleasant, yet it may not be surely kept from departing when it will. It is plain then how wretched is the happiness of mortal life which neither endures for ever with men of calm mind, nor ever wholly delights the care-ridden. Wherefore, then, O mortal men, seek ye that happiness without, which lies within yourselves? Ye are confounded by error and ignorance. I will shew you as shortly as I may, the pole on which turns the highest happiness. Is there aught that you value more highly than your own self? You will answer that there is nothing. If then you are master of yourself, you will be in possession of that which you will never wish to lose, and which Fortune will never be able to take from you. Yet consider this further, that you may be assured that happiness cannot be fixed in matters of chance: if happiness is the highest good of a man who lives his life by reason, and if that which can by any means be snatched away, is not the highest good (since that which is best cannot be snatched away), it is plain that Fortune by its own uncertainty can never come near to reaching happiness. Further, the man who is borne along by a happiness which may stumble, either knows that it may change, or knows it not: if he knows it not, what happiness can there be in the blindness of ignorance? If he knows it, he must needs live in fear of losing that which he cannot doubt that he may lose; wherefore an ever-present fear allows not such an one to be happy. Or at any rate, if he lose it without unhappiness, does he not think it worthless? For that, whose loss can be calmly borne, is indeed a small good. You, I know well, are firmly persuaded that men's understandings can never die; this truth is planted deep in you by many proofs: since then it is plain that the happiness of fortune is bounded by the death of the body, you cannot doubt that, if death can carry away happiness, the whole race of mortals is sinking into wretchedness to be found upon the border of death. But we know that many have sought the enjoyment of happiness not only by death, but even by sorrow and sufferings: how then can the presence of this life make us happy, when its end cannot make us unhappy?

He that would build on a lasting resting-place; who would be firm to resist the blasts of the storming wind; who seeks, too, safety where he may contemn the surge and threatening of the sea; must leave the lofty mountain's top, and leave the thirsting sands. The hill is swept by all the might of the headstrong gale: the sands dissolve, and will not bear the load upon them. Let him fly the danger in a lot which is pleasant rest unto the eye: let him be mindful to set his house surely upon the lowly rock. Then let the wind bellow, confounding wreckage in the sea, and thou wilt still be founded upon unmoving peace, wilt be blessed in the strength of thy defence: thy life will be spent in calmness, and thou mayest mock the raging passions of the air.

But now,' she continued, the first remedies of reasoning are reaching you more deeply, and I think I should now use those that are somewhat stronger. If the gifts of Fortune fade not nor pass quickly away, even so, what is there in them which could ever be truly yours, or which would not lose its value when examined or thought upon?

Are riches valuable for their own nature, or on account of your and other men's natures? Which is the more valuable, the gold itself or the power of the stored up money? Surely wealth shines more brightly when spent than when put away in masses. Avarice ever brings hatred, while generous spending brings honour. But that cannot remain with one person which is handed over to another: therefore money becomes valuable to its possessor when, by being scattered, it is transferred to others, and ceases to be possessed. And if all that is heaped together among mankind comes to one man, it makes the others all poor. A voice indeed fills equally the ears of all that hear: but your riches cannot pass to others without being lessened: and when they pass, they make poor those whom they leave. How strait then and poor are those riches, which most men may not have, and which can only come to one by making others poor!

Think again of precious stones: does their gleam attract your eyes? But any excellence they have is their own brilliance, and belongs not to men: wherefore I am amazed that men so strongly admire them. What manner of thing can that be which has no mind to influence, which has no structure of parts, and yet can justly seem to a living, reasoning mind to be beautiful? Though they be works of their creator, and by their own beauty and adornment have a certain low beauty, yet are they in rank lower than your own excellence, and have in no wise deserved your admiration.

Does the beauty of landscape delight you?'

Surely, for it is a beautiful part of a beautiful creation: and in like manner we rejoice at times in the appearance of a calm sea, and we admire the sky, the stars, the sun, and the moon.

Does any one of these,' said she, concern you? Dare you boast yourself of the splendid beauty of any one of such things? Are you yourself adorned by the flowers of spring? Is it your richness that swells the fruits of autumn? Why are you carried away by empty rejoicing. Why do you embrace as your own the good things which are outside yourself? Fortune will never make yours what Nature has made to belong to other things. The fruits of the earth should doubtless serve as nourishment for living beings, but if you would satisfy your need as fully as Nature needs, you need not the abundance of Fortune. Nature is content with very little, and if you seek to thrust upon her more than is enough, then what you cast in will become either unpleasing or even harmful

Again, you think that you appear beautiful in many kinds of clothing. But if their form is pleasant to the eyes, I would admire the nature of the material or the skill of the maker. Or are you made happy by a long line of attendants? Surely if they are vicious, they are but a burden to the house, and full of injury to their master himself; while if they are honest, how can the honesty of others be counted among your possessions?

Out of all these possessions, then, which you reckon as your wealth, not one can really be shown to be your own. For if they have no beauty for you to acquire, what have they for which you should grieve if you lose them, or in keeping which you should rejoice? And if they are beautiful by their own nature, how are you the richer thereby? For these would have been pleasing of themselves, though cut out from your possessions. They do not become valuable by reason that they have come into your wealth; but you have desired to count them among your wealth, because they seemed valuable. Why then do you long for them with such railing against Fortune? You seek, I believe, to put want to flight by means of plenty. But you find that the opposite results. The more various is the beauty of furniture, the more helps are needed to keep it beautiful; and it is ever true that they who have much, need much; and on the other hand, they need least who measure their wealth by the needs of nature, not by excess of display.

Is there then no good which belongs to you and is implanted within you, that you seek your good things elsewhere, in things without you and separate from you? Have things taken such a turn that the animal, whose reason gives it a claim to divinity, cannot seem beautiful to itself except by the possession of. lifeless trappings? Other classes of things are satisfied by their intrinsic possessions; but men, though made like God in understanding, seek to find among the lowest things adornment for their higher nature: and you do not understand that you do a great wrong thereby to your Creator. He intended that the human race should be above all other earthly beings; yet you thrust down your honourable place below the lowest.

For if every good thing is allowed to be more valuable than that to which it belongs, surely you are putting yourselves lower than them in your estimation, since you think precious the most worthless of things; and this is indeed a just result. Since, then, this is the condition of human nature, that it surpasses other classes only when it realises what is in itself; as soon as it ceases to know itself, it must be reduced to a lower rank than the beasts. To other animals ignorance of themselves is natural; in men it is a fault. How plainly and how widely do you err by thinking that anything can be adorned by ornaments that belong to others! Surely that cannot be. For if anything becomes brilliant by additions thereto, the praise for the brilliance belongs to the additions. But the subject remains in its own vileness, though hidden and covered by these externals.

Again, I say that naught can be a good thing which does harm to its possessor. Am I wrong? "No," you will say. Yet many a time do riches harm their possessors, since all base men, who are therefore the most covetous, think that they themselves alone are worthy to possess all gold and precious stones. You therefore, who now go in fear of the cudgel and sword of the robber, could laugh in his face if you had entered upon this path with empty pockets. [18] How wonderful is the surpassing blessing of mortal wealth! As soon as you have acquired it, your cares begin!

O happy was that early age of men, contented with their trusted and unfailing fields, nor ruined by the wealth that enervates. Easily was the acorn got that used to satisfy their longwhile fast. They knew not Bacchus' gifts, nor honey mixed therewith. They knew not how to tinge with Tyre's purple dyes the sheen of China's silks. Their sleep kept health on rush and grass; the stream gave them to drink as it flowed by: the lofty pine to them gave shade. Not one of them yet clave the ocean's depths, nor, carrying stores of merchandise, had visited new shores. Then was not heard the battle's trump, nor had blood made red with bitter hate the bristling swords of war. For why should any madness urge to take up first their arms up on an enemy such ones as knew no sight of cruel wounds nor knew rewards that could be reaped in blood? Would that our times could but return to those old ways! but love of gain and greed of holding burn more fiercely far than Ætna's fires. Ah! who was the wretch who first unearthed the mass of hidden gold, the gems that only longed to lie unfound? For full of danger was the prize he found.

What am I to say of power and of the honours of office, which you raise to heaven because you know not true honoured power? What fires belched forth from Ætna's flames, what overwhelming flood could deal such ruin as these when they fall into the hands of evil men? I am sure you remember how your forefathers wished to do away with the consular power, which had been the very foundation of liberty, because of the overbearing pride of the consuls, just as your ancestors had too in earlier times expunged from the state the name of king on account of the same pride. But if, as rarely happens, places of honour are granted to honest men, what else is delightful in them but the honesty they practise thereby? Wherefore honour comes not to virtue from holding office, but comes to office from virtues there practised.

But what is the power which you seek and esteem so highly? O creatures of the earth, can you not think over whom you are set? If you saw in a community of mice, one mouse asserting his rights and his power over the others, with what mirth you would greet the sight! Yet if you consider the body, what can you find weaker than humanity? Cannot a tiny gnat by its bite, or by creeping into the inmost parts, kill that body? How can any exercise right upon any other except upon the body alone, or that which is below the body, whereby I mean the fortunes? Can you ever impose any law upon a free spirit? Can you ever disturb the peculiar restfulness which is the property of a mind that hangs together upon the firm basis of its reason? When a certain tyrant thought that by tortures he would compel a free man [19] to betray the conspirators in a plot against his life, the philosopher bit through his tongue and spat it out in the tyrant's face. Thus were the tortures, which the tyrant intended to have cruel results, turned by the philosopher into subjects of high courage. Is there aught that one man can do to another, which he may not suffer from another in his turn? We have heard how Busiris, who used to kill strangers, was killed by Hercules when he came to Egypt. Regulus, [20] who had cast into chains many a Carthaginian captive, soon yielded himself a prisoner to their chains. Do you think that power to be any power, whose possessor cannot ensure his own escape from suffering at another's hands what he inflicts upon some other?

Further, if there were any intrinsic good in the nature of honours and powers themselves, they could never crowd upon the basest men. For opposites will not be bound together. Nature refuses to allow contraries to be linked to each other. Wherefore, while it is undoubted that for the most part offices of honour are enjoyed by bad men, it is also manifest that those things are not by nature good, which allow themselves to cling to evil men. And this indeed may worthily be held of all the gifts of fortune which come with the greatest success to the most unscrupulous. And in this matter we must also think on this fact, that no one doubts a man to be brave in whom he has found by examination that bravery is implanted: and whoever has the quality of swiftness is plainly swift. So also music makes men musical, medicine makes men physicians, oratory makes men orators. The nature of each quality acts as is peculiar to itself: it is not confused with the results of contrary qualities, but goes so far as to drive out those qualities which are opposed to it. Wealth cannot quench the insatiable thirst of avarice: nor can power ever make master of himself the man whom vicious passions hold fast in unbreakable chains. Honours, when joined to dishonest men, so far from making them honour- able, betray them rather, and show them to be dishonourable. Why is this so? It is because you rejoice to call things by false names which belong not to them--their names are refuted by the reality of their qualities: wherefore neither riches, nor that kind of power, nor these honours, can justly so be called. Lastly, we may come to the same conclusion concerning all the aspects of Fortune: nothing is to be sought in her, and it is plain she has no innate good, for she is not always joined with good men, nor does she make good those with whom she is joined.'

We have heard what ruin Nero wrought when Rome was burnt and senators were slain. We know how savagely he did to death his brother, [21] how he was stained by the spilling of his own mother's blood, and how he looked upon her cold body and yet no tear fell upon his cheek: yet could this man be judge of the morals that were dead. Nay, he was ruler of the peoples whom the sun looks upon from the time he rises in the east until he hides his rays beneath the waves, and those whom the chilling northern Wain o'errules, and those whom the southern gale burns with its dry blast, as it heats the burning sands. Say, could great power chasten Nero's maddened rage? Ah! heavy fate, how often is the sword of high injustice given where is already most poisonous cruelty!'

Then I said, You know that the vain-glory of this world has had but little influence over me; but I have desired the means of so managing affairs that virtue might not grow aged in silence.'

Yes,' said she, but there is one thing which can attract minds, which, though by nature excelling, yet are not led by perfection to the furthest bounds of virtue; and that thing is the love of fame and reputation for deserving well of one's country. Think then thus upon it, and see that it is but a slight thing of no weight. As you have learnt from astronomers' shewing, the whole circumference of the earth is but as a point compared with the size of the heavens. That is, if you compare the earth with the circle of the universe, it must be reckoned as of no size at all. And of this tiny portion of the universe there is but a fourth part, as you have learnt from the demonstration of Ptolemæus, [22] which is inhabited by living beings known to us. If from this fourth part you imagine subtracted all that is covered by sea and marsh, and all the vast regions of thirsty desert, you will find but the narrowest space left for human habitation. And do you think of setting forth your fame and publishing your name in this space, which is but as a point within another point so closely circumscribed? And what size or magnificence can fame have which is shut in by such close and narrow bounds? Further, this narrow enclosure of habitation is peopled by many races of men which differ in language, in customs, and in their whole scheme of living; and owing to difficulty of travelling, differences of speech, and rareness of any intercourse, the fame of cities can not reach them, much less the fame of men. Has not Cicero written somewhere that in his time the fame of Rome had not reached the mountains of the Caucasus, though the Republic was already well grown and striking awe among the Parthians and other nations in those parts? Do you see then how narrow and closely bounded must be that fame which you wish to extend more widely? Can the fame of a Roman ever reach parts to which the name of Rome cannot come?

  Further, the manners and customs of different races are so little in agreement, that what is make his name known, because he takes pleasure in a glorious fame. So each man shall be content if his fame travels throughout his own countrymen, and the immortality of his name shall be bounded by the limits of one nation. But how many men, the most famous of their times, are wiped out by oblivion because no man has written of them! [23] And yet what advantage is there in much that is written? For with their authors these writings are overwhelmed in the length and dimness of age. Yet when you think upon your fame in future ages, you seem to think that you are prolonging it to immortality. But if you think upon the unending length of eternity, what enjoyment do you find in the long endurance of your name? For though one moment bears but the least proportion to ten thousand years, yet there is a definite ratio, because both are limited spaces of time. But even ten thousand years, or the greatest number you will, cannot even be compared with eternity. For there will always be ratio between finite things, but between the finite and the infinite there can never be any comparison. Wherefore, however long drawn out may be the life of your fame, it is not even small, but it is absolutely nothing when compared with eternity. You k now not how to act rightly except for the breezes of popular opinion and for the sake of empty rumours; thus the excellence of conscience and of virtue is left behind, and you seek rewards from the tattle of other men. Listen to the witty manner in which one played once upon the shallowness of this pride. A certain man once bitterly attacked another who had taken to himself falsely the name of philosopher, not for the purpose of true virtue, but for pride of fame; he added to his attack that he would know soon whether he was a philosopher, when he saw whether the other bore with meekness and patience the insults he heaped upon him. The other showed patience for a while and took the insults as though he scoffed at them, until he said, "Do you now see that I am a philosopher?" "I should have, had you kept silence," said the other stingingly. But we are speaking of great men: and I ask, what do they gain from fame, though they seek glory by virtue? what have they after the body is dissolved at death? For if men die utterly, as our reason forbids us to believe, there is no glory left to them at all, since they whose it is said to be, do not exist. If, on the other hand, the mind is still conscious and working when it is freed from its earthly prison, it seeks heaven in its freedom and surely spurns all earthly traffic: it enjoys heaven and rejoices in its release from the of this world.

The mind that rushes headlong in its search for fame, thinking that is its highest good, should look upon the spreading regions of the air, and then upon the bounded tracts that are this world: then will shame enter it; that, though fame grow, yet can it never fill so small a circle. Proud men! why will ye try in vain to free your necks from the yoke mortality has set thereon? Though fame may be wide scattered and find its way through distant lands, and set the tongues there talking; though a splendid house may draw brilliance from famous names and tales; yet death regards not any glory, howsoever great. Alike he overwhelms the lowly and the lofty head, and levels high with low.

Where are Fabricius's [24] bones, that honourable man? What now is Brutus? [25] or unbending Cato? [26] Their fame survives in this: it has no more than a few slight letters shewing forth an empty name. We see their noble names engraved, and only know thereby that they are brought to naught. Ye lie then all unknown, and fame can give no knowledge of you. But if you think that life can be prolonged by the breath of mortal fame, yet when the slow time robs you of this too, then there awaits you but a second death.

But,' she said, do not think that I would urge implacable war upon Fortune. There are times when her deception of men has certain merits: I mean when she discovers herself, unveils her face, and proclaims her ways. Perhaps you do not yet understand what I would say. It is a strange thing that I am trying to say, and for that reason I can scarcely explain myself in words. I think that ill fortune is of greater advantage to men than good fortune. Good fortune is ever lying when she seems to favour by an appearance of happiness. Ill fortune is ever true when by her changes she shews herself inconstant. The one deceives; the other edifies. The one by a deceitful appearance of good things enchains the minds of those who enjoy them: the other frees them by a knowledge that happiness is so fragile. You see, then, that the one is blown about by winds, is ever moving and ever ignorant of its own self; the other is sober, ever prepared and ever made provident by the undergoing of its very adversities. Lastly, good fortune draws men from the straight path of true good by her fawning: ill fortune draws most men to the true good, and holds them back by her curved staff.

And do you think that this should be reckoned among the least benefits of this rough, unkind, and terrible ill fortune, that she has discovered to you the minds of your faithful friends? Fortune has distinguished for you your sure and your doubtful friends; her departure has taken away her friends and left you yours. At what price could you have bought this benefit if you had been untouched and, as you thought, fortunate? Cease then to seek the wealth you have lost. You have found your friends, and they are the most precious of all riches.

Through Love [27] the universe with constancy makes changes all without discord: earth's elements, though contrary, abide in treaty bound: Phoebus in his golden car leads up the glowing day; his sister rules the night that Hesperus brought: the greedy sea confines its waves in bounds, lest the earth's borders be changed by its beating on them: all these are firmly bound by Love, which rules both earth and sea, and has it s empire in the heavens too. If Love should slacken this its hold, all mutual love would change to war; and these would strive to undo the scheme which now their glorious movements carry out with trust and with accord. By Love are peoples too kept bound to-

BOETHIUS

gether by a treaty which they may not break. Love binds with pure affection the sacred tie of wedlock, and speaks its bidding to all trusty friends. O happy race of mortals, if your hearts are ruled as is the universe, by Love! [28]

[15] The proverbially rich and happy king; defeated and condemned to death by Cyrus, king of Media, in 546 B.C., but spared by him.

[16] The last king of Macedonia, defeated at Pydna, 168 B. C., by L. Æmilius Paulus.

[17] Boethius's first wife was Elpis, daughter of Festus: his second was Rusticiana, daughter of Symmachus, a senator and consul, A.D. 485. His second wife was the mother of the two sons mentioned below. (See Appendix, p. 169.)

[18] This is an application of Juvenal's lines (Sat. x. 19) which contrast the terror of the money-laden traveller with the careless happiness of the man who meets highwayman with no purse and empty pockets.

[19] This story is told of Anaxagoras and Nicocreon, king of Cyprus, c. B.C. 323.

[20] Regulus was the Roman general in Sicily in the first Punic War, taken prisoner in 255 B.C., and put to death in 250.

[21] Britannicus, son of Nero's father, the Emperor Claudius, put to death A.D. 55.

[22] A mathematician, astronomer, and geographer of Alexandria. Fl. 140-160 A.D. Boethius translated one of his works.

[23] Boethius is thinking of Horace, Odes iv. 9.
Ere Agamemnon saw the light,
There lived brave men: but tearless all
Enfolded in eternal night,
For lack of sacred minstrels, fall. (Mr. Gladstone's translation.)

[24] Fabricius was the Roman general whom Pyrrhus could neither bribe nor intimidate, B.C. 280.

[25] L. Junius Brutus, who led the Romans to expel the last of the kings, and was elected the first consul, B.C. 509.

[26] Probably Cato Major, the great censor, B.C. 184, the rigid champion of the stern old Roman morals; or possibly Cato Minor, who committed suicide at Utica after the battle of Thapsus, B.C. 46, because he considered that Cæsar's victory was fatal to the Republic and the liberty of Rome.

[27] Boethius in this passage is probably thinking of Empedocles's doctrine of Love which unites, and Strife which divides, the two primal forces in the universe.

[28] Cp. Bk. I. Prose iv, p. 10.

BOOK III

When she finished her lay, its soothing tones left me spellbound with my ears alert in my eagerness to listen. So a while afterwards I said, Greatest comforter of weary minds, how have you cheered me with your deep thoughts and sweet singing too! No more shall I doubt my power to meet the blows of Fortune. So far am I from terror at the remedies which you did lately tell me were sharper, that I am longing to hear them, and eagerly I beg you for them.'

Then said she, I knew it when you laid hold upon my words in silent attention, and I was waiting for that frame of mind in you, or more truly, I brought it about in you. They that remain are indeed bitter to the tongue, but sweet to the inner man. But as you say you are eager to hear, how ardently you would be burning, if you knew whither I am attempting to lead you!'

Whither is that?' I asked.

To the true happiness, of which your soul too dreams; but your sight is taken up in imaginary views thereof, so that you cannot look upon itself.'

Then said I, I pray you shew me what that truly is, and quickly.'

I will do so,' she said, for your sake willingly. But first I will try to picture in words and give you the form of the cause, which is already better known to you, that so, when that picture is perfect and you turn your eyes to the other side, you may recognise the form of true happiness.

When a man would sow in virgin soil, first he clears away the bushes, cuts the brambles and the ferns, that the corn-goddess may go forth laden with her new fruit. The honey, that the bee has toiled to give us, is sweeter when the mouth has tasted bitter things. The stars shine with more pleasing grace when a storm has ceased to roar and pour down rain. After the morning star has dispersed the shades of night, the day in all its beauty drives its rosy chariot forth. So thou hast looked upon false happiness first; now draw thy neck from under her yoke: so shall true happiness now come into thy soul.'

She lowered her eyes for a little while as though searching the innermost recesses of her mind; and then she continued: -- The trouble of the many and various aims of mortal men bring them much care, and herein they go forward by different paths but strive to reach one end, which is happiness. And that good is that, to which if any man attain, he can desire nothing further. It is that highest of all good things, and it embraces in itself all good things: if any good is lacking, it cannot be the highest good, since then there is left outside it something which can be desired. Wherefore happiness is a state which is made perfect by the union of all good things. This end all men seek to reach, as I said, though by different paths. For there is implanted by nature in the minds of men a desire for the true good; but error leads them astray towards false goods by wrong paths.

Some men believe that the highest good is to lack nothing, and so they are at pains to possess abundant riches. Others consider the true good to be that which is most worthy of admiration, and so they strive to attain to places of honour, and to be held by their fellow-citizens in honour thereby. Some determine that the highest good lies in the highest power; and so they either desire to reign themselves, or try to cleave to those who do reign. Others think that renown is the greatest good, and they therefore hasten to make a famous name by the arts of peace or of war. But more than all measure the fruit of good by pleasure and enjoyment, and these think that the happiest man is abandoned to pleasure.

Further, there are those who confuse the aims and the causes of these good things: as those who desire riches for the sake of power or of pleasure, or those who seek power for the sake of money or celebrity. In these, then, and other things like to them, lies the aim of men's actions and prayers, such as renown and popularity, which seem to afford some fame, or wife and children, which are sought for the pleasure they give. On the other hand, the good of friends, which is the most honourable and holy of all, lies not in Fortune's but in Virtue's realm. All others are adopted for the sake of power or enjoyment.

Again, it is plain that the good things of the body must be accounted to those false causes which we have mentioned; for bodily strength and stature seem to make men more able and strong; beauty and swiftness seem to give renown; health seems to give pleasure. By all these happiness alone is plainly desired. For each man holds that to be the highest good, which he seeks before all others. But we have defined the highest good to be happiness. Wherefore what each man desires above all others, he holds to be a state of happiness.

Wherefore you have each of these placed before you as the form of human happiness: wealth, honours, power, glory, and pleasure. Epicurus [29] considered these forms alone, and accordingly determined upon pleasure as the highest good, because all the others seemed but to join with it in bringing enjoyment to the mind.

But to return to the aims of men: their minds seem to seek to regain the highest good, and their memories seem to dull their powers. It is as though a drunken man were seeking his home, but could not remember the way thither. Can those people be altogether wrong whose aim it is to lack nothing? No, there is nothing which can make happiness so perfect as an abundant possession of good things, needing naught that belongs to others, but in all ways sufficing for itself. Surely those others too are not mistaken who think that what is best is also most worthy of reverence and respect. It cannot be any cheap or base thing, to attain which almost all men aim and strive. And is power not to be accounted a good thing? Surely it is: can that be a weak thing or forceless, which is allowed in all cases to excel? Is renown of no value? We cannot surrender this; that whatever is most excellent, has also great renown. It is hardly worth saying that happiness has no torturing cares or gloom, and is not subject to grief and trouble; for even in small things, the aim is to find that which it is a delight to have and to enjoy. These, then, are the desires of men: they long for riches, places of honour, kingdoms, glory, and pleasure; and they long for them because they think that thereby they will find satisfaction, veneration, power, renown, and happiness. It is the good then which men seek by their different desires; and it is easy to shew how great a force nature has put therein, since in spite of such varying and discordant opinions, they are all agreed in the goal they seek, that of the highest good.

I would to pliant strings set forth a song of how almighty Nature turns her guiding reins, telling with what laws her providence keeps safe this boundless universe, binding and tying each and all with cords that never shall be loosed. The lions of Carthage, though they bear the gorgeous bonds and trappings of captivity, and eat the food that is given them by hand, and though they fear their harsh master with his lash they know so well; yet if once blood has touched their bristling jaws, their old, their latent wills return; with deep roaring they remember their old selves; they loose their bands and free their necks, and their tamer is the first torn by their cruel teeth, and his blood is poured out by their rage and wrath.

If the bird who sings so lustily upon the high tree-top, be caught and caged, men may minister to him with dainty care, may give him cups of liquid honey and feed him with all gentleness on plenteous food; yet if he fly to the roof of his cage and see the shady trees he loves, he spurns with his foot the food they have put before him; the woods are all his sorrow calls for, for the woods he sings with his sweet tones.

The bough which has been downward thrust by force of strength to bend its top to earth, so soon as the pressing hand is gone, looks up again straight to the sky above.

Phoebus sinks into the western waves, but by his unknown track he turns his car once more to his rising in the east.

All things must find their own peculiar course again, and each rejoices in his own return. Not one can keep the order handed down to it, unless in some way it unites its rising to its end, and so makes firm, immutable, its own encircling course.

And you too, creatures of the earth, do dream of your first state, though with a dim idea. With whatsoever thinking it may be, you look to that goal of happiness, though never so obscure your thoughts: thither, to true happiness, your natural course does guide you, and from the same your various errors lead you. For I would have you consider whether men can reach the end they have resolved upon, namely happiness, by these ways by which they think to attain thereto. If money and places of honour and such-like do bring anything of that sort to a man who seems to lack no good thing, then let us acknowledge with them that men do become happy by the possession of these things. But if they cannot perform their promises, and there is still lack of further good things, surely it is plain that a false appearance of happiness is there discovered. You, therefore, who had lately abundant riches, shall first answer me. With all that great wealth, was your mind never perturbed by torturing care arising from some sense of injustice?'

Yes,' I said, I cannot remember that my mind was ever free from some such care.'

Was it not because something was lacking, which you missed, or because something was present to you which you did not like to have?'

Yes,' I answered.

You desired, then, the presence of the one, and the absence of the other?'

I acknowledge it.'

Then,' said she, such a man lacks what he desires.'

He does.'

But while a man lacks anything, can he possibly satisfy himself?'

No,' said I.

Then, while you were bountifully supplied with wealth, you felt that you did not satisfy yourself?'

I did indeed.'

Then,' said she, wealth cannot prevent a man from lacking or make him satisfied. And this is what it apparently professed to do. And this point too I feel is most important: money has in itself, by its own nature, nothing which can prevent its being carried off from those, who possess it, against their will.'

It has not,' I said.

No, you cannot deny that any stronger man may any day snatch it from them. For how come about the quarrels of the law-courts? Is it not because people try to regain money that has been by force or by fraud taken from them?' Yes,' I answered.

Then,' said she, a man will need to seek from the outside help to guard his own money.'

That cannot be denied,' I said.

And a man will not need that unless he possesses money which he can lose.'

Undoubtedly he will not.'

Then the argument turns round the other way,' she said. The riches which were thought to make a man all-sufficient for himself, do really put him in need of other people's help. Then how can need be separated from wealth? Do the rich never feel hunger nor thirst? Do the limbs of moneyed men never feel the cold of winter? You will say, "Yes, but the rich have the wherewithal to satisfy hunger and thirst, and drive away cold." But though riches may thus console wants, they cannot entirely take them away. For, though these ever crying wants, these continual requests, are satisfied, yet there must exist that which is to be satisfied. I need not say that nature is satisfied with little, greed is never satisfied. Wherefore, I ask you, if wealth cannot remove want, and even creates its own wants, what reason is there that you should think it affords satisfaction to a man?

Though the rich man with greed heap up from ever-flowing streams the wealth that cannot satisfy, though he deck himself with pearls from the Red Sea's shore, and plough his fertile field with oxen by the score, yet gnawing care will never in his lifetime leave him, and at his death his wealth will not go with him, but leave him faithlessly.'

But,' I urged, places of honour make the man, to whom they fall, honoured and venerated.'

Ah!' she answered, have those offices their force in truth that they may instil virtues into the minds of those that hold them, and drive out vices therefrom? And yet we are too well accustomed to see them making wickedness conspicuous rather than avoiding it. Wherefore we are displeased to see such places often falling to the most wicked of men, so that Catullus called Nonius "a diseased growth," [30] though he sat in the highest chair of office. Do you see how great a disgrace high honours can add to evil men? Their unworthiness is less conspicuous if they are not made famous by honours. Could you yourself have been induced by any dangers to think of being a colleague with Decoratus, [31] when you saw that he had the mind of an unscrupulous buffoon, and a base informer? We cannot consider men worthy of veneration on account of their high places, when we hold them to be unworthy of those high places. But if you see a man endowed with wisdom, you cannot but consider him worthy of veneration, or at least of the wisdom with which he is endowed. For such a man has the worth peculiar to virtue, which it transmits directly to those in whom it is found. But since honours from the vulgar crowd cannot create merit, it is plain that they have not the peculiar beauty of this worth. And here is a particular point to be noticed: if men are the more worthless as they are despised by more people, high position makes them all the worse because it cannot make venerable those whom it shews to so many people to be contemptible. And this brings its penalty with it: wicked people bring a like quality into their positions, and stain them with their infection.

Now I would have you consider the matter thus, that you may recognise that true veneration cannot be won through these shadowy honours. If a man who had filled the office of consul many times in Rome, came by chance into a country of barbarians, would his high position make him venerated by the barbarians? Yet if this were a natural quality in such dignities, they would never lose their effective function in any land, just as fire is never aught but hot in all countries. But since they do not receive this quality of veneration from any force peculiar to themselves, but only from a connexion in the untrustworthy opinions of men, they become as nothing as soon as they are among those who do not consider these dignities as such.

But that is only in the case of foreign peoples. Among the very peoples where they had their beginnings, do these dignities last for ever? Consider how great was the power in Rome of old of the office of Præfect: now it is an empty name and a heavy burden upon the income of any man of Senator's rank.' The præfect then, who was commissioner of the corn-market, was held to be a great man. Now there is no office more despised. For, as I said before, that which has no intrinsic beauty, sometimes receives a certain glory, sometimes loses it, according to the opinion of those who are concerned with it. If then high offices cannot make men venerated, if furthermore they grow vile by the infection of bad men, if changes of time can end their glory, and, lastly, if they are held cheaply in the estimation of whole peoples, I ask you, so far from affording true beauty to men, what beauty have they in themselves which men can desire?

Though Nero decked himself proudly with purple of Tyre and snow-white gems, none the less that man of rage and luxury lived ever hated of all. Yet would that evil man at times give his dishonoured offices to men who were revered. Who then could count men blessed, who to such a villain owed their high estate?

Can kingdoms and intimacies with kings make people powerful? "Certainly," some Thee may answer, "in so far as their happiness is lasting." But antiquity and our times too are full of examples of the contrary; examples of men whose happiness as kings has been exchanged for disaster. What wonderful power, which is found to be powerless even for its own preservation! But if this kingly power is really a source of happiness, surely then, if it fail in any way, it lessens the happiness it brings, and equally causes unhappiness. However widely human empires may extend, there must be still more nations left, over whom each king does not reign. And so, in whatever direction this power ceases to make happy, thereby comes in powerlessness, which makes men unhappy; thus therefore there must be a greater part of unhappiness in every king's estate. That tyrant 1 had learnt well the dangers of his lot, who likened the fear which goes with kingship to the terror inspired by a sword ever hanging overhead. What then is such a power, which cannot drive away the bite of cares, nor escape the stings of fear?

Yet these all would willingly live without fear, but they cannot, and yet they boast of their power. Think you a man is powerful when you see that he longs for that which he cannot bring to pass? Do you reckon a man powerful who walks abroad with dignity and attended by servants? A man who strikes fear into his subjects, yet fears them more himself? Damocles, what it was to be a tyrant, by setting him in his own seat at a sumptuous banquet,' but hung a sword above him by a hair. A man who must be at the mercy of those that serve him, in order that he may seem to have power?

Need I speak of intimacies with kings when kingship itself is shewn to be full of weakness? Not only when kings' powers fall are their friends laid low, but often even when their powers are intact. Nero compelled his friend and tutor, Seneca, [32] to choose how he would die. Papinianus, [33] for a long while a powerful courtier, was handed over to the soldiers' swords by the Emperor Antoninus. Yet each of these was willing to surrender all his power. Seneca even tried to give up all his wealth to Nero, and to seek retirement. But the very weight of their wealth and power dragged them down to ruin, and neither could do what he wished.

What then is that power, whose possessors fear it? in desiring to possess which, you are not safe, and from which you cannot escape, even though you try to lay it down? What help are friends, made not by virtue but by fortune? The friend gained by good fortune becomes an enemy in ill-fortune. And what plague can more effectually injure than an intimate enemy?

The man who would true power gain, must needs subdue his own wild thoughts: never must he let his passions triumph and yoke his neck by their foul bonds. For though the earth, as far as India's shore, tremble before the laws you give, though Thule bow to your service on earth's farthest bounds, yet if thou canst not drive away black cares, if thou canst not put to flight complaints, then is no true power thine.

How deceitful is fame often, and how base a thing it is! Justly did the tragic poet cry out, [34] "O Fame, Fame, how many lives of men Of naught hast thou puffed up! " For m any men have got a great name from the false opinions of the crowd. And what could be baser than such a thing? For those who are falsely praised, must blush to hear their praises. And if they are justly won by merits, what can they add to the pleasure of a wise man's conscience? For he measures his happiness not by popular talk, but by the truth of his conscience. If it attracts a man to make his name widely known, he must equally think it a shame if it be not made known. But I have already said that there must be yet more lands into which the renown of a single man can never come; wherefore it follows that the man, whom you think famous, will seem to have no such fame in the next quarter of the earth.

Popular favour seems to me to be unworthy even of mention under this head, for it comes not by any judgment, and is never constant.

Again, who can but see how empty a name, and how futile, is noble birth? For if its glory is due to renown, it belongs not to the man. For the glory of noble birth seems to be praise for the merits of a man's forefathers. But if praise creates the renown, it is the renowned who are praised. Wherefore, if you have no renown of your own, that of others cannot glorify you. But if there is any good in noble birth, I conceive it to be this, and this alone, that the highborn seem to be bound in honour not to show any degeneracy from their fathers' virtue.

From like beginning rise all men on earth, for there is one Father of all things; one is the guide of everything. 'Tis He who gave the sun his rays, and horn s unto the moon. 'Tis He who set mankind on earth, and in the heavens the stars. He put within our bodies spirits which were born in heaven. And thus a highborn race has He set forth in man. Why do ye men rail on your forefathers? If ye look to your be ginning and your author, which is God, is any man degenerate or base but he who by his own vices cherishes base things and leaves that beginning which was his?

And now what am I to say of the pleasures of the body? The desires of the flesh are full of cares, their fulfilment is full of remorse. What terrible diseases, what unbearable griefs, truly the fruits of sin, do they bring upon the bodies of those who enjoy them! I know not what pleasure their impulse affords, but any who cares to recall his indulgences of his passions, will know that the results of such pleasures are indeed gloomy. If any can shew that those results are blest with happiness, then may the beasts of the field be justly called blessed, for all their aims are urged toward the satisfying of their bodies' wants. The pleasures of wife and children may be most honourable; but nature makes it all too plain that some have found torment in their children. How bitter is any such kind of suffering, I need not tell you now, for you have never known it, nor have any such anxiety now. Yet in this matter I would hold with my philosopher Euripides, [35] that he who has no children is happy in his misfortune.

All pleasures have this way: those who enjoy them they drive on with stings. Pleasure, like the winged bee, scatters its honey sweet, then flies away, and with a clinging sting it strikes the hearts it touches.

CONSOLATION OF PHILOSOPHY

There is then no doubt that these roads to happiness are no roads, and they cannot lead any man to any end whither they profess to take him. I would shew you shortly with what great evils they are bound up. Would you heap up money? You will need to tear it from its owner. Would you seem brilliant by the glory of great honours? You must kneel before their dispenser, and in your desire to surpass other men in honour, you must debase yourself by setting aside all pride. Do you long for power? You will be subject to the wiles of all over whom you have power, you will be at the mercy of many dangers. You seek fame? You will be drawn to and fro among rough paths, and lose all freedom from care. Would you spend a life of pleasure? Who would not despise and cast off such servitude to so vile and brittle a thing as your body? How petty are all the aims of those who put before themselves the pleasures of the body, how uncertain is the possession of such? In bodily size will you ever surpass the elephant? In strength will you ever lead the bull, or in speed the tiger? Look upon the expanse of heaven, the strength with which it stands, the rapidity with which it moves, and cease for a while to wonder at base things. This heaven is not more wonderful for those things than for the design which guides it. How sweeping is the brightness of outward form, how swift its movement, yet more fleeting than the passing of the flowers of spring. But if, as Aristotle says, many could use the eyes of lynxes to see through that which meets the eye, then if they saw into the organs within, would not that body, though it had the most fair outside of Alcibiades, [36] seem most vile within? Wherefore it is not your own nature, but the weakness of the eyes of them that see you, which makes you seem beautiful. But consider how in excess you desire the pleasures of the body, when you know that howsoever you admire it, it can be reduced to nothing by a three-days' fever. To put all these points then in a word: these things cannot grant the good which they promise; they are not made perfect by the union of all good things in them; they do not le ad to happiness as a path thither; they do not make men blessed. [37]

Ah! how wretched are they whom ignorance leads astray by her crooked path! Ye seek not gold upon green trees, nor gather precious stones from vines, nor set your nets on mountain tops to catch the fishes for your feast, nor hunt the Umbrian sea in search of goats. Man knows the depths of the sea themselves, hidden though they be beneath its waves; he knows which water best yields him pearls, and which the scarlet dye. But in their blindness men are content, and know not where lies hid the good which they desire. They sink in earthly things, and there they seek that which has soared above the star-lit heavens. What can I call down upon them worthy of their stubborn folly? They go about in search of wealth and honours; and only when they have by labours vast stored up deception for themselves, do they at last know what is their true good.

So far,' she continued, we have been content to set forth the form of false happiness. If you clearly understand that, my next duty is to shew what is true happiness.'

I do see,' said I, that wealth cannot satisfy, that power comes not to kingdoms, nor veneration to high offices; that true renown cannot accompany ambition, nor true enjoyment wait upon the pleasures of the body.'

Have you grasped the reasons why it is so?' she asked.

I seem to look at them as through a narrow chink, but I would learn more clearly from you.'

The reason is to hand,' said she; human error takes that which is simple and by nature impossible to divide, tries to divide it, and turns its truth and perfection into falsity and imperfection. Tell me, do you think that anything which lacks nothing, can be without power?'

Of course not.'

You are right; for if anything has any weakness in any part, it must lack the help of something else.'

That is so,' I said.

Then perfect satisfaction and power have the same nature?'

Yes, it seems so.'

And do you think such a thing contemptible, or the opposite, worthy of all veneration?'

There can be no doubt that it is worthy.'

Then let us add veneration to that satisfaction and power, and so consider these three as one.'

Yes, we must add it if we wish to proclaim the truth.'

Do you then think that this whole is dull and of no reputation, or renowned with all glory? For consider it thus: we have granted that it lacks nothing, that it has all power and is worthy of all veneration; it must not therefore lack the glory which it cannot supply for itself, and thereby seem to be in any direction contemptible.'

No,' I said, I must allow that it has glory too.'

Therefore we must rank this glory equally with the other three.'

Yes, we must.'

Then that which lacks nothing from outside itself, which is all-powerful by its own might, which has renown and veneration, must surely be allowed to be most happy too?'

I cannot imagine from what quarter unhappiness would creep into such a thing, wherefore we must grant that it is full of happiness if the other qualities remain existent.'

Then it follows further, that though perfect satisfaction, power, glory, veneration, and happiness differ in name, they cannot differ at all in essence?'

They cannot.'

This then,' said she, is a simple, single thing by nature, only divided by the mistakes of base humanity; and while men try to gain a part of that which has no parts, they fail both to obtain a fraction, which cannot exist, and the whole too after which they do not strive.'

Tell me how they fail thus,' I said.

One seeks riches by fleeing from poverty, and takes no thought of power,' she answered, and so he prefers to be base and unknown, and even deprives himself of natural pleasures lest he should part with the riches which he has gathered. Thus not even that satisfaction reaches the man who loses all power, who is stabbed by sorrow, lowered by his meanness, hidden by his lack of fame. Another seeks power only: he scatters his wealth, he despises pleasures and honours which have no power, and sets no value upon glory. You see how many things such an one lacks. Sometimes he goes without necessaries even, sometimes he feels the bite and torture of care; and as he cannot rid himself of these, he loses the power too which he sought above all things. The same argument may be applied to offices, glory, and pleasure. For since each one of these is the same as each other, any man who seeks one without the others, gains not even that one which he desires.'

What then?' I asked.

If any man desires to obtain all together, he will be seeking the sum of happiness. But will he ever find that in these things which we have shewn cannot supply what they promise?' No.'

Then happiness is not to be sought for among these things which are separately believed to supply each thing so sought.'

Nothing could be more plainly true,' I said.

Then you have before you the form of false happiness, and its causes; now turn your attention in the opposite direction, and you will quickly see the true happiness which I have promised to shew you.'

But surely this is clear even to the blindest, and you shewed it before when you were trying to make clear the causes of false happiness. For if I mistake not, true and perfect happiness is that which makes a man truly satisfied, powerful, venerated, renowned, and happy. And (for I would have you see that I have looked deeply into the matter) I realise without doubt that that which can truly yield any one of these, since they are all one, is perfect happiness.

Ah! my son,' said she, I do see that you are blessed in this opinion, but I would have you add one thing.'

What is that?' I asked.

Do you think that there is anything among mortals, and in our perishable lives, which could yield such a state?'

I do not think that there is, and I think that you have shewn this beyond the need of further proof.'

These then seem to yield to mortals certain appearances of the true good, or some such imperfections; but they cannot give true and perfect good.'

No.'

Since, then, you have seen what is true happiness, and what are the false imitations thereof, it now remains that you should learn whence this true happiness may be sought.'

For that,' said I, I have been impatiently waiting.'

But divine help must be sought in small things as well as great (as my pupil Plato says in his Timoeus); [38] so what, think you, must we do to deserve to find the place of that highest good?'

Call,' I said, upon the Father of all, for if we do not do so, no undertaking would be rightly or duly begun.'

You are right,' said she; and thus she cried aloud: -- [39]

Thou who dost rule the universe with everlasting law, founder of earth and heaven alike, who hast bidden time stand forth from out Eternity, for ever firm Thyself, yet giving movement unto all. No causes were without Thee which could thence impel Thee to create this mass of changing matter, but within Thyself exists the very idea of perfect good, which grudges naught, for of what can it have envy? Thou makest all things follow that high pattern. In perfect beauty Thou movest in Thy mind a world of beauty, making all in a like image, and bidding the perfect whole to complete its perfect functions. All the first principles of nature Thou dost bind together by perfect orders as of numbers, so that they may be balanced each with its opposite: cold with heat, and dry with moist together; thus fire may not fly upward too swiftly because too purely, nor may the weight of the solid earth drag it down and overwhelm it. Thou dost make the soul as a third between mind and material bodies: to these the soul gives life and movement, for Thou dost spread it abroad among the members of the universe, now working in accord. Thus is the soul divided as it takes its course, making two circles, as though a binding thread around the world. Thereafter it returns unto itself and passes around the lower earthly mind; and in like manner it gives motion to the heavens to turn their course. Thou it is who dost carry forward with like inspiration these souls and lower lives. Thou dost fill these weak vessels with lofty souls, and send them abroad throughout the heavens and earth, and by Thy kindly law dost turn them again to Thyself and bring them to seek, as fire doth, to rise to Thee again.

Grant then, O Father, that this mind of ours may rise to Thy throne of majesty; grant us to reach that fount of good. Grant that we may so find light that we may set on Thee unblinded eyes; cast Thou therefrom the heavy clouds of this material world. Shine forth upon us in Thine own true glory. Thou art the bright and peaceful rest of all Thy children that worship Thee. To see Thee clearly is the limit of our aim. Thou art our beginning, our progress, our guide, our way, our end.

Since then you have seen the form both of the imperfect and the perfect good, I think I should now shew you where lies this perfection of happiness. In this I think our first inquiry must be whether any good of this kind can exist in the very nature of a subject; for we must not let any vain form of thought make us miss the truth of this matter. But there can be no denial of its existence, that it is as the very source of all good. For if anything is said to be imperfect, it is held to be so by some loss of its perfection. Wherefore if in any kind of thing a particular seems imperfect, there must also be a perfect specimen in the same kind. For if you take away the perfection, it is impossible even to imagine whence could come the so-called imperfect specimen. For nature does not start from degenerate or imperfect specimens, but starting from the perfect and ideal, it degenerates to these lower and weaker forms. If then, as we have shewn above, there is an uncertain and imperfect happiness to be found in the good, then there must doubtless be also a sure and perfect happiness therein.'[40]

Yes,' said I, that is quite surely proved to be true.'

Now consider,' she continued, where it lies. The universally accepted notion of men proves that God, the fountain-head of all things, is good. For nothing can be thought of better than God, and surely He, than whom there is nothing better, must without doubt be good. Now reason shews us that God is so good, that we are convinced that in Him lies also the perfect good. For if it is not so, He cannot be the fountain-head; for there must then be something more excellent, possessing that perfect good, which appears to be of older origin than God: for it has been proved that all perfections are of earlier origin than the imperfect specimens of the same: wherefore, unless we are to prolong the series to infinity, we must allow that the highest Deity must be full of the highest, the perfect good. But as we have laid down that true happiness is perfect good, it must be that true happiness is situated in His Divinity.' Yes, I accept that; it cannot be in any way contradicted.'

But,' she said, I beg you, be sure that you accept with a sure conscience and determination this fact, that we have said that the highest Deity is filled with the highest good.'

How should I think of it?' I asked.

You must not think of God, the Father of all , whom we hold to be filled with the highest good, as having received this good into Himself from without, nor that He has it by nature in such a manner that you might consider Him, its possessor, and the happiness possessed, a s having different essential existences. For if you think that good ha s been received from without, that which gave it must be more excellen t than that which received it; but we have most rightly stated that He is the most excellent of all things. And if you think that it is in Him by His nature, but different in kind, then, while we speak of God as the fountain-head of all things, who could imagine by whom these different kinds can have been united? Lastly, that which is different from anything cannot be the thing from which it differs. So anything which is by its nature different from the highest good, cannot be the highest good. And this we must not think of God, than whom there is nothing more excellent, as we have agreed. Nothing in this world can have a nature which is better than its origin, wherefore I would conclude that that which is the origin of all things, according to the truest reasoning, is by its essence the highest good.'

Most truly,' I said.

BOETHIUS

You agree that the highest good is happiness?'

Yes.'

Then you must allow that God is absolute happiness?'

I cannot deny what you put forward before, and I see that this follows necessarily from those propositions.'

Look then,' she said, whether it is proved more strongly by this too: there cannot be two highest goods which are different. For where two good things are different, the one cannot be the other; wherefore neither can be the perfect good, while each is lacking to the other. And that which is not perfect cannot be the highest, plainly. Therefore if two things are highest good, they cannot be different. Further, we have proved to ourselves that both happiness and God are each the highest good. Therefore the highest Deity must be identical with the highest happiness.'

No conclusion,' I said, could be truer in fact, or more surely proved by reason, or more worthy of our God.'

Besides this let me give you corollary, as geometricians do, when they wish to add a point drawn from the propositions they have proved. Since men become happy by acquiring happiness, and happiness is identical with divinity, it is plain that they become happy by acquiring divinity. But just as men become just by acquiring the quality of justice, and wise by wisdom, so by the same reasoning, by acquiring divinity they become divine. Every happy man then is divine. But while nothing prevents as many men as possible from being divine, God is so by His nature, men become so by participation.'

This corollary,' I said, or whatever you call it, is indeed beautiful and very precious.'

Yes, but nothing can be more beautiful than this too which reason would have us add to what we have agreed upon.'

What is that?' I asked.

Happiness seems to include many things: do all these join it together as into a whole which is happiness, as though each thing were a different part thereof, or is any one of them a good which fulfils the essence of happiness, and do the others merely bear relations to this one?'

'I would have you make this plain by the enunciation of these particulars.'

'Do we not,' she asked, 'hold that happiness is a good thing?'

'Yes,' I answered, 'the highest good.'

'But you may apply this quality of happiness to them all. For the perfect satisfaction is the same, and the highest power, and veneration, and renown, and pleasure; these are all held to be happiness.'

'What then?' I asked.

'Are all these things, satisfaction, power, and the others, as it were, members of the body, happiness, or do they all bear their relation to the good, as members to a head?'

'I understand what you propose to examine, but I am waiting eagerly to hear what you will lay down.'

'I would have you take the following explanation,' she said. 'If these were all members of the one body, happiness, they would differ individually. For this is the nature of particulars, to make up one body of different parts. But all these have been shewn to be one and the same. Therefore they are not as members; and further, this happiness will then appear to be joined together into a whole body out of one member, which is impossible.'

'That is quite certain,' said I, 'but I would hear what is to come.'

'It is plain that the others have some relation to the good. It is for that reason, namely because it is held to be good, that this satisfaction is sought, and power likewise, and the others too; we may suppose the same of veneration, renown, and pleasure. The good then is the cause of the desire for all of these, and their consummation also. Such a thing as has in itself no real or even pretended good, cannot ever be sought. On the other hand, such things as are not by nature good, but seem to be so, are sought as though they were truly good. Wherefore we may justly believe that their good quality is the cause of the desire for them, the very hinge on which they turn, and their consummation. The really important object of a desire, is that for the sake of which anything is sought, as a means. For instance, if a man wishes to ride for the sake of his health, he does not so much desire the motion of riding, as the effect, namely health. As, therefore, each of these things is desired for the sake of the good, the absolute good is the aim, rather than themselves. But we have agreed that the other things are desired for the sake of happiness, wherefore in this case too, it is happiness alone which is the object of the desire. Wherefore it is plain that the essence of the good and of happiness is one and the same.'

I cannot see how any one can think otherwise.'

But we have shewn that God and true happiness are one and the same.'

Yes.'

Therefore,' said she, we may safely conclude that the essence of God also lies in the absolute good and nowhere else.

Come hither all who are the prey of passions, bound by their ruthless chains; those deceiving passions which blunt the minds of men. Here shall you find rest from your labours; here a haven lying in tranquil peace; this shall be a resting-place open to receive within itself all the miserable on earth. Not all the wealth of Tagus's golden sands, nor Hermus's gleaming strand, [41] nor Indus, nigh earth's hottest zone, mingling its emeralds and pearls, can bring light to the eyes of any soul, but rather plunge the soul more blindly in their shade. In her deepest caverns does earth rear all that pleases the eye and excites the mind. The glory by which the heavens move and have their being, has nought to do with the darknesses which bring ruin to the soul. Whosoever can look on this true light will scarce allow the sun's rays to be clear.'

I cannot but agree with that,' I said, for it all stands woven together by the strongest proofs.' Then she said, At what would you value this, namely if you could find out what is the absolute good?'

'I would reckon it,' I said, at an infinite value, if I could find out God too, who is the good.'

'And that too I will make plain by most true reasoning, if you will allow to stand the conclusions we have just now arrived at.'

'They shall stand good.'

'Have I not shewn,' she asked, that those upon the things which most men seek are for this reason not perfect goods, because they differ between the highest themselves; they are lacking to one another, and so cannot afford full, absolute good? But when they are gathered together, as it were, into one form and one operation, so that complete satisfaction, power, veneration, renown, and pleasure are all the same, then they become the true good. Unless they are all one and the same, they have no claim to be reckoned among the true object s of men's desires.'

'That has been proved beyond all doubt.'

'Then such things as differ among themselves are not goods, but they become so when they begin to be a single unity. Is it not then the ca se these become goods by the attainment of unity?'

'Yes,' I said, it seems so.'

'But I think you allow that every good is good by participation in good?'

'Yes, I do.'

'Then by reason of this likeness both unity and good must be allowed to be the same thing; for such things as have by nature the same operation, have the same essence.'

'Undeniably.'

'Do you realise that everything remains existent so long as it keeps its unity, but perishes in dissolution as soon as it loses its unity?'

'How so?' I asked.

In the case of animals,' she said, so long as mind and body remain united, you have what you call an animal. But as soon as this unity is dissolved by the separation of the two, the animal perishes and can plainly be no longer called an animal. In the case of the body, too, so long as it remains in a single form by the union of its members, the human figure is presented. But if the division or separation of the body's parts drags that union asunder, it at once ceases to be what it was. In this way one may go through every subject, and it will be quite evident that each thing exists individually, so long as it is one, but perishes so soon as it ceases to be one.'

Yes, I see the same when I think of other cases.'

Is there anything,' she then asked, which, in so far as it acts by nature, ever loses its desire for self-preservation, and would voluntarily seek to come to death and corruption?'

No,' I said; while I think of animals which have volition in their nature, I can find in them no desire to throw away their determination to remain as they are, or to hasten to perish of their own accord, so long as there are no external forces compelling them thereto. Every animal labours for its preservation, shunning death and extinction. But about trees and plants, I have great doubts as to what I should agree to in their case, and in all inanimate objects.'

But in this case too,' she said, you have no reason to be in doubt, when you see how trees and plants grow in places which suit them, and where, so far as nature is able to prevent it, they cannot quickly wither and perish. For some grow in plains, others on mountain s; some are nourished by marshes, others cling to rocks; some are fertilised by otherwise barren sands, and would wither away if one tried to transplant them to better soil. Nature grants to each what suits it, and works against their perishing while they can possibly remain alive. I need hardly remind you that all plants seem to have their mouths buried in the earth, and so they suck up nourishment by their roots and diffuse their strength through their pith and bark: the pith being the softest part is always hidden away at the heart and covered, protected, as it were, by the strength of the wood; while outside, the bark, as being the defender who endures the best, is opposed to the unkindness of the weather. Again, how great is nature's care, that they should all propagate themselves by the reproduction of their seed; they all, as is so well known, are like regular machines not merely for lasting a time, but for reproducing themselves for ever, and that by their own kinds. Things too which are supposed to be inanimate, surely do all seek after their own by a like process. For why is flame carried upward by its lightness, while solid things are carried down by their weight, unless it be that these positions and movements are suitable to each? Further, each thing preserves what is suitable to itself, and what is harmful, it destroys. Hard things, such as stones, cohere with the utmost tenacity of their parts, and resist easy dissolution; while liquids, water, and air, yield easily to division, but quickly slip back to mingle their parts which have been cut asunder. And fire cannot be cut at all.

We are not now discussing the voluntary movements of a reasoning mind, but the natural instinct. For instance, we unwittingly digest the food we have eaten, and unconsciously breathe in sleep. Not even in animals does this love of self-preservation come from mental wishes, but from elementary nature. For often the will, under stress of external causes, embraces the idea of death, from which nature revolts in horror. [42] And, on the other hand, the will sometimes restrains what nature always desires, namely the operation of begetting, by which alone the continuance of mortal things becomes enduring. Thus far, then, this love of self-preservation arises not from the reasoning animal s intention, but from natural instinct. Providence h as given to its creatures this the greatest cause of permanent existence, the instinctive desire to remain existent so far as possible. Wherefore you have no reason to doubt that all things, which exist, seek a permanent existence by nature, and similarly avoid extinction.'

Yes,' I said, I confess that I see now beyond all doubt what appeared to me just now uncertain.'

But,' she continued, that which seeks to continue its existence, aims at unity; for take this away, and none will have any chance of continued existence.'

That is true.'

Then all things desire unity,' she said, and I agreed.

But we have shewn unity to be identical with the good?'

BOETHIUS

Yes,' said I.

Then all things desire the good; and that you may define as being the absolute good which is desired by all.'

Nothing could be more truthfully reasoned. For either everything is brought back to nothing, and all will flow on at random with no guiding head; or if there is any universal aim, it will be the sum of all good.'

Great is my rejoicing, my son,' said she, for you have set firmly in your mind the mark of the central truth. And hereby is made plain to you that which you a short time ago said that you knew not.'

What was that?'

What was the final aim of all things,' she said, for that is plainly what is desired by all: since we have agreed that that is the good, we must confess that the good is the end of all things.

If any man makes search for truth with all his penetration, and would be led astray by no deceiving paths, let him turn upon himself the light of an inward gaze, let him bend by force the long-drawn wanderings of his thoughts into one circle; let him tell surely to his soul, that he has, thrust away within the treasures of his mind, all that he labours to acquire without. Then shall that truth, which now was hid in error's darkening cloud, shine forth more clear than Phoebus's self. For the body, though it brings material mass which breeds forgetfulness, has never driven forth all light from the mind. The seed of truth does surely cling within, and can be roused as a spark by the fanning of philosophy. For if it is not so, how do ye men make answers true of your own instinct when teachers question you? Is it not that the quick spark of truth lies buried in the heart's low depths? And if the Muse of Plato sends through those depths the voice of truth, each man has not forgotten and is but reminding himself of what he learns.' [43] When she made an end, I said, I agree very strongly with Plato; for this is the second time that you have reminded me of these thoughts. The first time I had lost them through the material influence of the body; the second, when overwhelmed by this weight of trouble.'

'If,' said she, 'you look back upon what we that have agreed upon earlier, you will also soon recall what you just now said you knew not.'

'What is that?' I asked.

'The guidance by which the universe is directed.'

'Yes, I remember confessing my ignorance, and though I think I foresee the answer you will offer, I am eager to hear you explain it more fully.'

'This world,' she said, 'you thought a little while ago must without doubt be guided by God.'

'And I think so now,' I said, 'and will never think there is any doubt thereof; and I will shortly explain by what reasoning I arrive at that point. This universe would never have been suitably put together into one form from such various and opposite parts, unless there were some One who joined such different parts together; and when joined, the very variety of their natures, so discordant among themselves, would break their harmony and tear them asunder unless the One held together what it wove into one whole. Such a fixed order of nature could not continue its course, could not develop motions taking such various directions in place, time, operation, space, and attributes, unless there were One who, being immutable, had the disposal of these various changes. And this cause of their remaining fixed and their moving, I call God, according to the name familiar to all.'

Then said she, 'Since these are your feelings, I think there is but little trouble left me before you may revisit your home with happiness in your grasp. But let us look into the matter we have set before ourselves. Have we not shewn that complete satisfaction exists in true happiness, and we have agreed that God is happiness itself, have we not?'

'We have.'

'Wherefore He needs no external aid in governing the universe, or, if He had any such need, He would not have this complete sufficiency.'

That of necessity follows,' I said.

Then He arranges all things by Himself.'

Without doubt He does.'

And God has been shewn to be the absolute good.'

Yes, I remember.'

Then He arranges all things by good, if He arranges them by Himself, whom we have agreed to be the absolute good. And so this is the tiller and rudder by which the ship of the universe is kept sure and unbreakable.'

I feel that most strongly,' I said; and I foresaw that you would say so before, though I had a slight uncertainty.'

I believe you,' she said, 'for now you bring your eyes more watchfully to scan the truth. But what I am going to say is no less plain to the sight.'

What is that?'

Since we may reasonably be sure that God steers all things by the helm of goodness, and, as I have shewn you, all things have a natural instinct to hasten towards the good, can there be any doubt that they are guided according to their own will: and that of their own accord they turn to the will of the supreme disposer, as though agreeing with, and obedient to, the helmsman?'

That is so,' I said, and the government would not seem happy if it was a yoke upon discontented necks, and not the salvation of the submissive.'

Then nothing need oppose God's way for its own nature's preservation.'

No.'

But if it try to oppose Him, will it ever have any success at all against One whom we have justly allowed to be supremely powerful in matters of happiness?'

Certainly not.'

Then there is nothing which could have the will or the power to resist the highest good?'

I think not.'

Then it is the highest good which is guiding with strength and disposing with gentleness?'

Then said I, How great pleasure these things give me! not only those which have been proved by the strongest arguments, but still more the words in which you prove them, which make me ashamed that my folly has bragged so loudly.'

You have heard in mythology how the giants attacked heaven. It was this kindly strength which overthrew them too, as was their desert. But would you care to put these arguments at variance? For perhaps from such a friction, some fair spark of truth may leap forth.'

As you hold best,' I said.

Nobody would care to doubt that God is all-powerful?'

At any rate, no sane man would doubt it.'

Being, then, all-powerful, nothing is beyond His power?'

Nothing.'

Can, then, God do evil?'

No.'

Then evil is nothing, since it is beyond His power, and nothing is beyond His power?'

Are you playing with me,' I asked, weaving arguments as a labyrinth out of which I shall find no way? You may enter a labyrinth by the way by which you may come forth: come now forth by the way you have gone in: or are you folding your reason in some wondrous circle of divine simplicity? A little while ago you started from happiness, and said that happiness was the highest good; and you shewed how that rested in the highest Deity. And you reasoned that God too was the highest good, and the fullest happiness; and you allowed, as though granting a slight gift, that none could be happy except such as were similarly divine. Again, you said that the essence of God and of happiness was identical with the very form of good; and that that alone was good which was sought by all nature. And you argued, too, that God guided this universe by the helm of goodness; and that all creatures with free will obeyed this guidance, and that there was no such thing as natural evil; and all these things you developed by no help from without, but by homely and internal proofs, each gaining its credence from that which went before it.'

Then she answered, I was not mocking you. We have worked out the greatest of all matters by the grace of God, to whom we prayed. For the form of the divine essence is such that it is not diffused without, nor receives aught into itself from without. But as Parmenides says of it, "It is a mass well rounded upon all sides." [44] But if you examine it with reasoning, sought for not externally but by lying within the sphere of the very thing we are handling, you will not wonder at what you have learnt on Plato's authority, [45] that our language must be akin to the subjects of which we speak.

Happy the man who could reach the crystal fount of good: happy he who could shake off the chains of matter and of earth. The singer of Thrace in olden time lamented his dead wife: by his tearful strains he made the trees to follow him, and bound the flowing streams to stay: for him the hind would fearlessly go side by side with fiercest lions, and the hare would look upon the hound, nor be afraid, for he was gentle under the song's sway. But when the hotter flame burnt up his inmost soul, even the strains, which had subdued all other things, could not soothe their own lord's mind. Complaining of the hard hearts of the gods above, he dared approach the realms below. There he tuned his songs to soothing tones, and sang the lays he had drawn from his mother's [46] fount of excellence. His unrestrained grief did give him power, his love redoubled his grief's power: his mourning moved the depths of hell. With gentlest prayers he prayed to the lords of the shades for grace. The three-headed porter [47] was taken captive with amazement at his fresh songs. The avenging goddesses, [48] who haunt with fear the guilty, poured out sad tears. Ixion's [49] wheel no longer swiftly turned. Tantalus, [50] so long abandoned unto thirst, could then despise the flowing stream. The vulture, satisfied by his strains, tore not awhile at Tityos's [51] heart. At last the lord of the shades [52] in pity cried: "We are conquered; take your bride with you, bought by your song; but one condition binds our gift: till s he has left these dark abodes, turn not your eyes upon her." Who shall set a law to lovers? Love is a greater law unto itself. Alack! at the very bounds of darkness Orpheus looked upon his Eurydice; looked, and lost her, and was lost himself.

To you too this tale refers; you, who seek to lead your thoughts to the light above. For whosoever is overcome of desire, and turns his gaze upon the darkness neath the earth, he, while he looks on hell, loses the prize he carried off.'

[29] Epicurus (B.C. 342-270) was the famous founder of the Epicurean school of philosophy. His school had a large following of Romans under the Empire. His own teaching was of a higher nature than might be supposed from this bare statement that he thought pleasure was the highest good.'
[30] Probably Boethius makes a mistake in his interpretation of Catullus (Carm. 52), as Nonius's surname was very likely Struma' (which also means a wen); in which case Catullus cannot at most have intended more to be understood than a play upon the man's true name.
[31] Decoratus was a minion of Theodoric.
[32] Seneca, the philosopher and wise counsellor of Nero, was by him compelled to commit suicide, A.D. 65.
[33] Papinianus, the greatest lawyer of his time, was put to death by the Emperor Antoninus Caracalla, A.D. 212.
[34] Euripides, Andromache, 319-320.
[35] Referring to lines in the Andromache (419-420), where Euripides says: The man who complains that he has no children suffers less than he who has them, and is blest in his misfortune.'
[36] Alcibiades was the most handsome and brilliantly fascinating of all the public men of Athens in her most brilliant period.
[37] Compare Philosophy's first words about the highest good, p. 58.

[38] Plato, Timoeus, 27 C. (ch. v.) -- All those who have even the least share of moderation, on undertaking any enterprise, small or great, always call upon God at the beginning.'

[39] This hymn is replete with the highest development of Plato's theory of ideas, as expressed in the Timoeus, and his theory of the ideal good being the moving spirit of the material world. Compare also the speculative portion of Virgil, Æneid, vi.

[40] This reasoning hangs upon Plato's theory of ideas and so is the opposite of the theory of evolution.

[41] The modern Sarabat, in Asia Minor, formerly auriferous.

[42] Boethius is possibly thinking here of passages in Plato's Republic, Bk. iv. (439-441) where Socrates points out the frequent opposition of reason and instinct.

[43] Plato's doctrine of remembrance is chiefly treated of in his Phædo and Meno.

[44] This is a verse from the poems in which Parmenides embodied his philosophy: this was the doctrine of the unity which must have been in Boethius's mind above. Parmenides, the founder of the Eleatic school (495 B.C.) was perhaps, considering his early date, the greatest and most original of Greek philosophers. Boethius probably did not make a clear distinction between the philosopher's own poems and the views expressed in Plato's Parmenides.

[45] Plato in the Timoeus says, The language must also be akin to the subjects of which its words are the interpreters' -- (29 B.).

[46] Orpheus's mother was the Muse Calliope, mistress of the Castalian fount.

[47] The dog Cerberus.

[48] The Furies.

[49] Ixion for his crimes was bound upon a rolling wheel

[50] Tantalus for his crimes was condemned to perpetual hunger and thirst though surrounded by fruits and water which ever eluded his grasp.

[51] Tityos for his crimes was for ever fastened to the ground while a vulture devoured his entrails.

[52] Pluto.

BOOK IV

THUS gently sang the Lady Philosophy with dignified mien and grave countenance; and when she ceased, I, who had not thoroughly forgotten the grief with in me, interrupted her as she was about to speak further. Herald of true light,' I said, right clear have been the outpourings of your speech till now, seeming inspired as one contemplates them, and invincible through your reasonings. And though through grief for the injustices I suffer, I had forgotten them, yet you have not spoken of They what I knew not at all before. But this one thing is the chief cause of my grief, namely that, when there exists a good governor of the world, evils should exist at all, or, existing, should go unpunished. I would have you think how strange is this fact alone. But there is an even stranger attached thereto: ill-doing reigns and flourishes, while virtue not only lacks its reward, but is even trampled underfoot by wicked doers, and pays the penalties instead of crime. Who can wonder and complain enough that such things should happen under the rule of One who, while all-knowing and all-powerful, wills good alone?'

Then she answered: Yes, it would be most terrible, monstrous, and infinitely amazing if it were as you think. It would be as though in a well-ordered house of a good master, the vilest vessels were cared for while the precious were left defiled. But it is not so. If our former conclusions are unshaken, God Himself, of whose government we speak, will teach you that the good are always powerful, the evil are always the lowest and weakest; vice never goes unpunished; virtue never goes without its own reward; happiness comes to the good, misfortune to the wicked: and when your complaints are set at rest, many such things would most firmly strengthen you in this opinion. You have seen now from my teaching the form of true happiness; you know now its place: let us go quickly through all that must be lightly passed over, and let me shew you the road which shall lead you to your home. I will give wings to your mind, by which it shall raise itself aloft: so shall disquiet be driven away, and you may return safe to your home by my guidance, by the path I shall shew you, even by myself carrying you thither.

Yea, airy wings are mine to scale the heights of heaven; when these the min d has donned, swiftly she loathes and spurns this earth.

She soars above the sphere of this vast atmosphere, sees the clouds behind her far; she passes high above the topmost fires which seethe above the feverish turmoil of the air, [53] until she rises to the stars' own home, and joins her path unto the sun's; or accompanies on her path the cold and ancient Saturn, maybe as the shining warrior Mars; or she may take her course through the circle of every star that decks the night. And when she has had her fill of journeying, then may she leave the sky and tread the outer plane of the swift moving air, as mistress of the awful light. Here holds the King of kings His sway, and guides the reins of the universe, and Himself unmoved He drives His winged chariot, the bright disposer of the world. And if this path brings thee again hither, the path that now thy memory seeks to recall, I tell thee, thou shalt say, "This is my home, hence was I derived, here shall I stay my course." But if thou choose to look back upon the earthly night behind thee, thou shalt see as exiles from light the tyrants whose grimness made wretched peoples so to fear.'

Wondrous,' I cried; what vast things do you promise! and I doubt not that you can fulfil them. I only beg that you will not hold me back with delays, now that you have excited me thus far.'

First, then, you must learn that power is never lacking to the good, while the wicked are devoid of all strength. The proofs of these two statements hang upon each other. For good and bad are opposites, and therefore, if it is allowed that good is powerful, the weakness of evil is manifest: if the weakness and uncertainty of evil is made plain, the strength and sureness of good is proved. To gain more full credit for my opinion, I will go on to make my argument sure by first the one, then the other of the two paths, side by side.

It is allowed that there are two things upon which depend the entire operation of human actions: they are will and power. For if the will be wanting, a man does not even attempt that which he has no desire to perform; if the power be wanting, the will is exercised in vain. Wherefore, if you see a man wish for that which he will in no wise gain, you cannot doubt that he lacks the power to attain that which he wishes.'

That is plain beyond doubt.'

And if you see a man gain that which he wishes, can you doubt that he has the power?'

No.'

But wherein a man has power, he is strong; wherein he has not power, he must be counted weak?'

Yes.'

Do you remember that we agreed from our earlier reasonings, that the instinct of all human will, though acted upon by different aims, does lead with eagerness towards happiness?'

Yes,' said I, I remember that that too was proved.'

Do you remember that happiness is the absolute good, and that the good is desired of all, when in that manner happiness is sought?'

I need not recall that,' I said, since it is present fixedly in my memory.'

Then all men, good and bad alike, seek to arrive at the good by no different instincts?'

Yes, that follows necessarily.'

But it is certain that the good become so by the attainment of good?'

Yes.'

Then the good attain that which they wish?'

Yes,' said I, it seems so.'

But if evil men attain the good they seek, they cannot be evil?'

No.'

Since, then, both classes seek the good, which the good attain, but the evil attain not, it is plain that the good are powerful, while the evil are weak?'

If any doubt that, he cannot judge by the nature of the world, nor by the sequence of arguments.'

Again she said, If there are two persons before whom the same object is put by natural instinct, and one person carries his object through, working by his natural functions, but the other cannot put his natural instinct into practice, but using some function unsuitable to nature he can imitate the successful person, but not fulfil his original purpose, in this case, which of the two do you decide to be the more capable?'

I think I guess what you mean, but I would hear more explicitly.'

You will not, I think, deny that the motion of walking is a natural one to mankind?'

No, I will not.'

And is not that the natural function of the feet?'

Yes.'

If, then, one man walks, being able to advance upon his feet, while another, who lacks the natural function of feet, uses his hands and so tries to walk, which of these two may justly be held the more capable?'

Weave me other riddles!' I exclaimed, for can any one doubt that a man who enjoys his natural functions, is more capable than one who is incapable in that respect?'

But in the case of the highest good,' she said, it is equally the purpose set before good and bad men; good men seek it by the natural functions of virtue, while bad men seek to attain the same through their cupidity, which is not a natural function for the attainment of good. Think you not so?'

I do indeed,' said I; this is plain, as also is the deduction which follows. For it must be, from what I have already allowed, that the good are powerful, the wicked weak.'

Your anticipation is right; and as doctors are wont to hope, it shews a lively nature now fit to withstand disease. But I see that you are very ready in understanding, and I will multiply my arguments one upon another. See how great is the weakness of these wicked men who cannot even attain that to which their natural instinct leads them, nay, almost drives them. And further, how if they are deprived of this great, this almost invincible, aid of a natural instinct to follow? Think what a powerlessness possesses these men. They are no light objects which they seek; they seek no objects in sport, objects which it is impossible that they should achieve. They fail in the very highest of all things, the crown of all, and in this they find none of the success for which they labour day and night in wretchedness. But herein the strength of good men is conspicuous. If a man could advance on foot till he arrived at an utmost point beyond which there was no path for further advance, you would think him most capable of walking: equally so, if a man grasps the very end and aim of his search, you must think him most capable. Wherefore also the contrary is true; that evil men are similarly deprived of all strength. For why do they leave virtue and follow after vice? Is it from ignorance of good? Surely not, for what is weaker or less compelling than the blindness of ignorance? Do they know what they ought to follow, and are they thrown from the straight road by passions? Then they must be weak too in self-control if they cannot struggle with their evil passions. But they lose thus not only power, but existence all together. For those who abandon the common end of all who exist, must equally cease to exist. And this may seem strange, that we should say that evil men, though the majority of mankind, do not exist at all; but it is so. For while I do not deny that evil men are evil, I do deny that they "are," in the sense of absolute existence. You may say, for instance, that a corpse is a dead man, but you cannot call it a man. In a like manner, though I grant that wicked men are bad, I cannot allow that they are men at all, as regards absolute being. A thing exists which keeps its proper place and preserves its nature; but when anything falls away from its nature, its existence too ceases, for that lies in its nature. You will say, " Evil men are capable of evil": and that I would not deny. But this very power of theirs comes not from strength, but from weakness. They are capable of evil; but this evil would have no efficacy if it could have stayed under the operation of good men. And this very power of ill shews the more plainly that their power is naught. For if, as we have agreed, evil is nothing, then, since they are only capable of evil, they are capable of nothing.'

That is quite plain.'

I would have you understand what is this strength of power. We have a little while ago laid down that nothing is more powerful than the highest good?'

Yes,' I said.

But the highest good can do no evil?'

No.'

Is there any one who thinks that men are all-powerful?'

No one,' I said, unless he be mad.'

And yet those same men can do evil.'

Would to heaven they could not!' I cried.

Then a powerful man is capable only of all good; but even those who are capable of evil, are not capable of all: so it is plain that those who are capable of evil, are capable of less. Further, we have shewn that all power is to be counted among objects of desire, and all objects of desire have their relation to the good, as to the coping-stone of their nature. But the power of committing crime has no possible relation to the good. Therefore it is not an object of desire. Yet, as we said, all power is to be desired. Therefore the power of doing evil is no power at all. For all these reasons the power of good men and the weakness of evil men is apparent. So Plato's opinion [54] is plain that "the wise alone are able to do what they desire, but unscrupulous men can only labour at what they like, they cannot fulfil their real desires." They do what they like so long as they think that they will gain through their pleasures the good which they desire; but they do not gain it, since nothing evil ever reaches happiness.

Kings you may see sitting aloft upon their thrones, gleaming with purple, hedged about with g rim guarding weapons, threatening with fierce glances, and their hearts heaving with passion. If any man take from these proud ones their outward covering of empty honour, he will see within, will see that these great ones bear secret chains. For the heart of one is thus filled by lust with the poisons of greed, or seething rage lifts up its waves and lashes his mind therewith: or gloomy grief holds them weary captives, or by slippery hopes they are tortured. So when you see one head thus labouring beneath so many tyrants, you know he cannot do as he would, for by hard task-masters is the master himself oppressed.

Do you see then in what a slough crimes are involved, and with what glory honesty shines forth? It is plain from this that reward is never lacking to good deeds, nor punishment to crime. We may justly say that the reward of every act which is performed is the object for which it is performed. For instance, on the racecourse the crown for which the runner strives is his reward. But we have shewn that happiness is the identical good for the sake of which all actions are performed. Therefore the absolute good is the reward put before all human actions. But good men cannot be deprived of this. And further, a man who lacks good cannot justly be describe d as a good man; wherefore we may say that good habits never miss their rewards. Let the wicked rage never so wildly, the wise man's crown shall never fail nor wither. And the wickedness of bad men can never take aw ay from good men the glory which belongs to them. Whereas if a good man rejoiced in a glory which he received from outside, then could another, or even he, may be, who granted it, carry it away. But since honesty grants to every good man its own rewards, he will only lack his reward when he ceases to be good. And lastly, since every reward is sought for the reason that it is held to be good, who shall say that the man, who possesses goodness, does not receive his reward? And what reward is this? Surely the fairest and greatest of all. Remember that corollary [55] which I emphasised when speaking to you a little while ago; and reason thus therefrom. While happiness is the absolute good, it is plain that all good men become good by virtue of the very fact that they are good. But we agreed that happy men are as gods. Therefore this is the reward of the good, which no time can wear out, no power can lessen, no wickedness can darken; they become divine. In this case, then, no wise man can doubt of the inevitable punishment of the wicked as well. For good and evil are so set, differing from each other just as reward and punishment are in opposition to each other: hence the rewards, which we see fall to the good, must correspond precisely to the punishments of the evil on the other side. As, therefore, honesty is itself the reward of the honest, so wickedness is itself the punishment of the wicked. Now whosoever suffers punishment, doubts not that he is suffering an evil: if, then, they are ready so to judge of themselves, can they think that they do not receive punishment, considering that they are not only affected but thoroughly permeated by wickedness, the worst of all evils?

Then, from the other point of view of the good, see what a punishment ever goes with the wicked. You have learnt a little while past that all that exists is one, and that the good itself is one; it follows therefrom that all that exists must appear to be good. In this way, therefore, all that falls away from the good, ceases also to exist, wherefore evil men cease to be what they were. The form of their human bodies still proves that they have been men; wherefore they must have lost their human nature when they turned to evil-doing. But as goodness alone can lead men forward beyond their humanity, so evil of necessity will thrust down be low the honourable estate of humanity those whom it casts down from their first position. The result is that you cannot hold him to be a man who has been, so to say, transformed by his vices. If a violent man and a robber burns with greed of other men's possessions, you say he is like a wolf. Another fierce man is always working his restless tongue at lawsuits, and you will compare him to a hound. Does another delight to spring upon men from ambushes with hidden guile? He is as a fox. Does one man roar and not restrain his rage? He would be reckoned as having the heart of a lion. Does another flee and tremble in terror where there is no cause of fear? He would be held to be as deer. If another is dull and lazy, does he not live the life of an ass? One whose aims are inconstant and ever changed at his whims, is in no wise different from the birds. If another is in a slough of foul and filthy lusts, he is kept down by the lusts of an unclean swine. Thus then a man who loses his goodness, ceases to be a man, and since he cannot change his condition for that of a god, he turns into a beast.

The east wind wafted the sails which carried on the wandering ships of Ithaca's king to the island where dwelt the fair goddess Circe, the sun's own daughter. There for her new guests she mingled cups bewitched by charms. Her hand, well skilled in use of herbs, changed these guests to different forms. One bears the face of a boar; another grows like to an African lion with fangs and claws; this one becomes as a wolf, and when he thinks to weep, he howls; that one is an Indian tiger, though he walks all harmless round about the dwelling-place. The leader alone, Ulysses, though beset by so many dangers, was saved from the goddess's bane by the pity of the winged god, Mercury.

But the sailors had drunk of her cups, and now had turned from food of corn to husks and acorns, food of swine. Naught is left the same, speech and form are gone; only the mind remains unchanged, to bewail their unnatural sufferings.

How weak was that hand, how powerless those magic herbs which could change the limbs but not the he art! Within lies the strength of men, hidden in deep security. Stronger are those dread poisons which can drag a man out of himself, which work their way within: they hurt not the body, but on the mind their rage inflicts a grievous wound.' [56]

Then I answered: I confess that I think it is justly said that vicious men keep only the outward bodily form of their humanity, and, in the attributes of their souls, are changed to beasts. But I would never have allowed them willingly the power to rage in the ruin of good men through their fierce and wicked intentions.'

They have not that power,' said she, as I will shew you at a convenient time. But if this very power, which you believe is allowed to them, were taken from them, the punishment of vicious men would be to a great extent lightened. For, though some may scarcely believe it, evil men must be more unhappy when they carry out their ill desires than when they cannot fulfil them. For if it is pitiable to have wished bad things, it is more pitiable to have had the power to perform them, without which power the performance of this pitiable will would never have effect. Thus, when you see men with the will and the power to commit a crime, and you see them perform it, they must be the victims of a threefold misfortune, since each of those three things brings its own misery.

Yes,' said I, I agree; but I do wish from my heart that they may speedily be rid of one of these misfortunes, being deprived of this power of doing evil.'

They will be rid of it,' she said, more speedily even than you wish perhaps, and sooner than they think they will be rid thereof. There is in the short course of life naught which is so long coming that an immortal mind can think it has long to wait for it. Many a time are their high hopes and great plans for evil-doing cut short by a sudden and unlooked-for end. This indeed it is that sets a limit to their misery.

For if wickedness makes a man miserable, the longer he is wicked, the more miserable must he be; and I should hold them most miserable of all, if not even death at last put an end to their evil-doing. If we have reached true conclusions concerning the unhappiness of depravity, the misery, which is said to be eternal, can have no limit.'

That is a strange conclusion and hard to accept. But I see that it is suited too well by what we have agreed upon earlier.'

You are right,' she said; but when one finds it hard to agree with a conclusion, one ought in fairness to point out some fault in the argument which has preceded, or shew that the sequence of statements is not so joined together as to effectively lead to the conclusion; otherwise, if the premises are granted, it is not just to cavil at the inference. This too, which I am about to say, may not seem less strange, but it follows equally from what has been taken as fact.'

What is that?' I asked.

That wicked men are happier when they pay the penalty for their wickedness than when they receive no penalty at the hands of justice. [57] I am not going to urge what may occur to any one, namely, that depraved habits are corrected by penalties, and drawn towards the right by fear of punishment, and that an example is hereby given to others to avoid all that deserves blame. But I think that the wicked who are not punished are in another way the more unhappy, without regard to the corrective quality of punishment, nor its value as an example.'

And what way is there other than these?'

We have allowed, have we not,' she said, that the good are happy, but the bad are miserable.'

Yes.'

Then if any good be added to the misery of any evil man, is he not happier than the man whose miserable state is purely and simply miserable without any good at all mingled therewith?'

I suppose so.'

What if some further evil beyond those by which a man, who lacked all good things, were made miserable, were added to his miseries? Should not he be reckoned far more unhappy than the man whose misfortune was lightened by a share in some good?'

Of course it is so.'

Therefore,' she said, the wicked when punished have something good added to their lot, to wit, their punishment, which is good by reason of its quality of justice; and they also, when unpunished, have something of further evil, their very impunity, which you have allowed to be an evil, by reason of its injustice.'

I cannot deny that,' said I.

Then the wicked are far more unhappy when they are unjustly unpunished, than when they are justly punished. It is plain that it is just that the wicked should be punished, and unfair that they should escape punishment.'

No one will gainsay you.'

But no one will deny this either, that all which is just is good; and on the other part, all that is unjust is evil.'

Then I said: The arguments which we have accepted bring us to that conclusion. But tell me, do you leave no punishment of the soul to follow after the death of the body?'

Yes,' she answered, heavy punishments, of which some, I think, are effected by bitter penalties, others by a cleansing mercy. [58] But it is not my intention to discuss these now. My object has been to bring you to know that the power of evil men, which seems to you so unworthy, is in truth nothing; and that you may see that those wicked men, of whose impunity you complained, do never miss the reward of their ill-doing; and that you may learn that their passion, which you prayed might soon be cut short, is not long-enduring, and that the longer it lasts, the more unhappiness it brings, and that it would be most unhappy if it endured for ever. Further, I have tried to shew you that the wicked are more to be pitied if they escape with unjust impunity, than if they are punished by just retribution. And it follows upon this fact that they will be undergoing heavier penalties when they are thought to be unpunished.'

When I hear your arguments, I feel sure that they are true as possible. But if I turn to human opinions, I ask what man would not think them not only incredible, but even unthinkable?'

Yes,' she said, 'for men cannot raise to the transparent light of truth their eyes which have been accustomed to darkness. They are like those birds whose sight is clear at night, but blinded by daylight. So long as they look not upon the true course of nature, but upon their own feelings, they think that the freedom of passion and the impunity of crime are happy things. Think upon the sacred ordinances of eternal law. If your mind is fashioned after better things, there is no need of a judge to award a prize; you have added yourself to the number of the more excellent. If your mind sinks to worse things, seek no avenger from without: you have thrust yourself downward to lower things. It is as though you were looking at the squalid earth and the heavens in turn; then take away all that is about you; and by the power of sight, you will seem to be in the midst now of mud, now of stars. But mankind looks not to such things. What then shall we do? Shall we join ourselves to those whom we have shewn to be as beasts? If a man lost utterly his sight, and even forgot that he had ever seen, so that he thought he lacked naught of human perfection, should we think that such a blind one can see as we do? Most people would not even allow another point, which rests no less firmly upon strong reasons, namely, that those who do an injury are more unhappy than those who suffer one.' [59]

I would hear those strong reasons,' I said.

You do not deny that every wicked man deserves punishment?'

No.'

It is plain for many reasons that the wicked are unhappy?'

Yes.'

Then you doubt not that those who are worthy of punishment are miserable?'

No, I agree.'

If then you were sitting as a judge, upon which would you consider punishment should fall -- the man who did the injury, or the man who suffered it?'

I have no hesitation in saying that I would make amends to the sufferer at the expense of the doer of the injustice.'

Then the doer of the injustice would seem to you more miserable than the sufferer?'

That follows.'

Then from this,' said she, and other causes which rest upon the same foundation, it is plain that, since baseness makes men more miserable by its own nature, the misery is brought not to the sufferer of an injustice, but to the doer thereof. But the speakers in law-courts take the opposite course: they try to excite the pity of the judges for those who have suffered any heavy or bitter wrong; but more justly their pity would be due to those who have committed the wrong. These guilty men ought to be brought, by accusers kindly rather than angry, to justice, as patients to a doctor, that their disease of crime may be checked by punishment. Under such an arrangement the occupation of advocates for defence would either come to a complete stand-still, or if it seemed more to the advantage of mankind, it might turn to the work of prosecution. And if the wicked too themselves might by some device look on virtue left behind them, and if they could see that they would lay aside the squalor of vice by the pain of punishment, and that they would gain the compensation of achieving virtue again, they would no longer hold it punishment, but would refuse the aid of advocates for their defence, and would intrust themselves unreservedly to their accusers and their judges. In this way there would be no place left for hatred among wise men. For who but the most foolish would hate good men? And the re is no cause to hate bad men. Vice is as a disease of the mind, just as feebleness shews ill-health in the body. As, then, we should never think that those, who are sick in the body, deserve hatred, so are those, whose minds are oppressed by a fiercer disease than feebleness, namely wickedness, much more worthy of pity than of persecution.

BOETHIUS

To what good end do men their passions raise, even to drag from fate their deaths by their own hands? If ye seek death, she is surely nigh of her own will; and her winged horses she will not delay. Serpents and lions, bears, tigers and boars, all seek your lives with their fangs, yet do ye seek them with swords? Is it because your manners are so wide in variance that men raise up unjust battles and savage wars, and seek to perish by each other's darts? Such is no just reason for this cruelty. Wouldst thou apportion merit to merit fitly? Then love good men as is their due, and for the evil shew your pity.'

Then said I, I see how happiness and misery lie inseparably in the deserts of good and bad men. But I am sure that there is some good and some bad in the general fortune of men. For no wise man even would wish to be exiled, impoverished, and disgraced rather than full of wealth, power, veneration, and strength, and flourishing securely in his own city. The operation of wisdom is shewn in this way more nobly and clearly, when the happiness of rulers is in a manner transmitted to the people who come into contact with their rule; and especially when prisons, bonds, and other penalties of the law become the lot of the evil citizens for whom they were designed. I am struck with great wonder why these dues are interchanged; why punishments for crimes fall upon the good, while the bad citizens seize the rewards of virtue; and I long to learn from you what reason can be put forward for such unjust confusion. I should wonder less if I could believe that everything was the confusion of accident and chance. But now the thought of God's guidance increases my amazement; He often grants happiness to good men and bitterness to the bad, and then, on the other hand, sends hardships to the good and grants the desires of the wicked. Can we lay our hands on any cause? If not, what can make this state different in any way from accidental chance?'

It is no wonder,' she answered, if one who knows not the order and reasons of nature, should think it is all at random and confused. But doubt not, though you know not the cause of such a great matter of the world's government, doubt not, I say, that all is rightly done, because a good Governor rules the universe.

If any man knows not that the star Arcturus [60] has his course nearest the topmost pole how shall he not be amazed that Boötes so slowly takes his wain and is so late to dip his brightness in the ocean, and yet so swiftly turns to rise again? The law of heaven on high will but bewilder him. When the full moon grows dim to its horns, darkened by the shadow of dull night, when Phoebe thus lays bare all the varying bands of the stars, which she had hidden by the power of her shining face: then are the nations stirred by the errors of the vulgar, and beat without ceasing brazen cymbals. [61] No man is surprised when the blasts of the wind beat a shore with roaring waves, nor when a solid mass of frozen snow is melted by the warmth of Phoebus's rays; for herein the causes are ready at hand to be understood. But in those other matters the causes are hidden, and so do trouble all men's hearts, for time does not grant them to advance with experience in such things as seldom recur: the common herd is ever amazed at all that is extraordinary. But let the cloudy errors of ignorance depart, and straightway these shall seem no longer marvellous.'

That is true,' I said; but it is your kind office to unravel the causes of hidden matters, and explain reasons now veiled in darkness; wherefore I beg of you, put forth your decree and expound all to me, since this wonder most deeply stirs my mind.'

Then said she, smiling, Your question calls me to the greatest of all these matters, and a full answer thereto is well-nigh impossible. For this is its kind: if one doubt be cut away, innumerable others arise, as the Hydra's heads; and there can be no limit unless a man restrains them by the most quick fire of the mind. For herein lie the questions of the directness of Providence, the course of Fate, chances which cannot be foreseen, knowledge, divine predestination, and freedom of judgment. You can judge for yourself the weight of these questions. But since it is a part of your treatment to know some of these, I will attempt to make some advantage therefrom, though we are penned in by our narrow space of time. But if you enjoy the delights of song, you must wait a while for that pleasure, while I weave together for you the chain of reasons.'

As you will,' said I. Then, as though beginning afresh, she spake thus:

The engendering of all things, the whole advance of all changing natures, and every motion and progress in the world, draw their causes, their order, and their forms from the allotment of the unchanging mind of God, which lays manifold restrictions on all action from the calm fortress of its own directness Such restrictions are called

Providence when they can be seen to lie in the very simplicity of divine understanding; but they were called Fate in old times when they were viewed with reference to the objects which they moved or arranged. It will easily be understood that these two are very different if the mind examines the force of each. For Providence is the very divine reason which arranges all things, and rests with the supreme disposer of all; while Fate is that ordering which is a part of all changeable things, and by means of which Providence binds all things together in their own order. Providence embraces all things equally, however different they may be, even however infinite: when they are assigned to their own places, forms, and times, Fate sets them in an orderly motion; so that this development of the temporal order, unified in the intelligence of the mind of God, is Providence. The working of this unified development in time is called Fate. These are different, but the one hangs upon the other. For this order, which is ruled by Fate, emanates from the directness of Providence. Just as when a craftsman perceives in his mind the form of the object he would make, he sets his working power in motion, and brings through the order of time that which he had seen directly and ready present to his mind. So by Providence does God dispose all that is to be done, each thing by itself and unchangeably; while these same things which Providence has arranged are worked out by Fate in many ways and in time. Whether, therefore, Fate works by the aid of the divine spirits which serve Providence, or whether it works by the aid of the soul, or of all nature, or the motions of the stars in heaven, or the powers of angels, or the manifold skill of other spirits, whether the course of Fate is bound together by any or all of these, one thing is certain, namely that Providence is the one unchangeable direct power which gives form to all things which are to come to pass, while Fate is the changing bond, the temporal order of those things which are arranged to come to pass by the direct disposition of God. Wherefore everything which is subject to Fate is also subject to Providence, to which Fate is itself subject. But there are things which, though beneath Providence, are above the course of Fate. Those things are they which are immovably set nearest the primary divinity, and are there beyond the course of the movement of Fate. As in the case of spheres moving round the same axis, that which is nearest the centre approaches most nearly the simple motion of the centre, and is itself, as it were, an axis around which turn those which are set outside it. That sphere which is outside all turns through a greater circuit, and fulfils a longer course in proportion as it is farther from the central axis; and if it be joined or connect itself with that centre, it is drawn into the direct motion thereof, and no longer strays or strives to turn away. In like manner, that which goes farther from the primary intelligence, is bound the more by the ties of Fate, and the nearer it approaches the axis of all, the more free it is from Fate. But that which clings without movement to the firm intellect above, surpasses altogether the bond of Fate. As, therefore, reasoning is to understanding; as that which becomes is to that which is; as time is to eternity; as the circumference is to the centre: so is the changing course of Fate to the immovable directness of Providence. That course of Fate moves the heavens and the stars, moderates the first principles in their turns, and alters their forms by balanced interchangings. The same course renews all things that are born and wither away by like advances of offspring and seed. It constrains, too, the actions and fortunes of men by an unbreakable chain of causes: and these causes must be unchangeable, as they proceed from the beginnings of an unchanging Providence. Thus is the world governed for the best if a directness, which rests in the intelligence of God, puts forth an order of causes which may not swerve. This order restrains by its own unchangeableness changeable things, which might otherwise run hither and thither at random. Wherefore in disposing the universe this limitation directs all for good, though to you who are not strong enough to comprehend the whole order, all seems confusion and disorder. Naught is there that comes to pass for the sake of evil, or due to wicked men, of whom it has been abundantly shewn that they seek the good, but misleading error turns them from the right course; for never does the true order, which comes forth from the centre of the highest good, turn any man aside from the right beginning.

But you will ask, "What more unjust confusion could exist than that good men should sometimes enjoy prosperity, sometimes suffer adversity, and that the bad too should sometimes receive what they desire, sometimes what they hate?" Are then men possessed of such infallible minds that they, whom they consider honest or dishonest, must necessarily be what they are held to be? No, in these matters human judgment is at variance with itself, and those who are held by some to be worthy of reward, are by others held worthy of punishment. But let us grant that a man could discern between good and bad characters. Can he therefore know the inmost feelings of the soul, as a doctor can learn a body's temperature? For it is no less a wonder to the ignorant why sweet things suit one sound body, while bitter things suit another; or why some sick people are aided by gentle draughts, others by sharp and bitter ones. But a doctor does not wonder at such things, for he knows the ways and constitutions of health and sickness. And what is the health of the soul but virtue? and what the sickness, but vice? And who is the preserver of the good and banisher of the evil, who but God, the guardian and healer of minds? God looks forth from the high watch-tower of His Providence, He sees what suits each man, and applies to him that which suits him. Hence then comes that conspicuous cause of wonder in the order of Fate, when a wise man does that which amazes the ignorant. For, to glance at the depth of God's works with so few words as human reason is capable of comprehending, I say that what you think to be most fair and most conducive to justice's preservation, that appears different to an all-seeing Providence. Has not our fellow-philosopher Lucan told us how "the conquering cause did please the gods, but the conquered, Cato?" [62] What then surprises you when done on this earth, is the true-guided order of things; it is your opinion which is perverted and confused. But if there is any one whose life is so good that divine and human estimates of him agree, yet he must be uncertain in the strength of his mind; if any adversity befall him, it may always be that he will cease to preserve his innocence, by which he found that he could not preserve his good fortune. Thus then a wise dispensation spares a man who might be made worse by adversity, lest he should suffer when it is not good for him to be oppressed. Another may be perfected in all virtues, wholly conscientious, and very near to God: Providence holds that it is not right such an one should receive any adversity, so that it allows him to be troubled not even by bodily diseases. As a better man [63] than I has said, "The powers of virtues build up the body of a good man." It often happens that the duty of a supreme authority is as signed to good men for the purpose of pruning the insolent growth of wickedness. To some, Providence grants a mingled store of good and bad, according to the nature of their minds. Some she treats bitterly, lest they grow too exuberant with long continued good fortune; others she allows to be harassed by hardships that the virtues of their minds should be strengthened by the habit and exercise of patience. Some have too great a fear of sufferings which they can bear; others have too great contempt for those which they cannot bear: these she leads on by troubles to make trial of themselves. Some have brought a name to be honoured for all time at the price of a glorious death. Some by shewing themselves undefeated by punishment, have left a proof to others that virtue may be invincible by evil. What doubt can there be of how rightly such things are disposed, and that they are for the good of those whom we see them befall? The other point too arises from like causes, that sometimes sorrows, sometimes the fulfilment of their desires, falls to the wicked. As concerns the sorrows, no one is surprised, because all agree that they deserve ill. Their punishments serve both to deter others from crime by fear, and also to amend the lives of those who undergo them; their happiness, on the other hand, serves as a proof to good men of how they should regard good fortune of this nature, which they see often attends upon the dishonest. And another thing seems to me to be well arranged: the nature of a man may be so headstrong and rough that lack of wealth may stir hi m to crime more readily than restrain him; for the disease of such an one Providence prescribes a remedy of stores of patrimony: he may see that his conscience is befouled by sin, he may take account with himself of his fortune, and will perhaps fear lest the loss of this property, of which he enjoys the use, may bring unhappiness. Wherefore he will change his ways, and leave off from ill-doing so long as he fears the loss of his fortune. Again, good fortune, unworthily improved, has flung some into ruin. To some the right of punishing is committed that they may use it for the exercise and trial of the good, and the punishment of evil men. And just as there is no league between good and bad men, so also the bad cannot either agree among themselves: nay, with their vices tearing their own consciences asunder, they cannot agree with themselves, and do often perform acts which, when done, they perceive that they should not have done. Wherefore high Providence has thus often shewn her strange wonder, namely, that bad men should make other bad men good. For some find themselves suffering injustice at the hands of evil men, and, burning with hatred of those who have injured them, they have returned to cultivate the fruits of virtue, because their aim is to be unlike those whom they hate. To divine power, and to that alone, are evil things good, when it uses them suitably so as to draw good results therefrom. For a definite order embraces all things, so that even when some subject leaves the true place assigned to it in the order, it returns to an order, though another, it may be, lest aught in the realm of Providence be left to random chance. But "ha rd is it for me to set forth all these matters as a god," [64] nor is it right for a man to try to comprehend with his mind all the means of divine working, or to explain them in words. Let it be enough that we have seen that God, the Creator of all nature, directs and disposes all things for good. And while He urges all, that He has made manifest, to keep His own likeness, He drives out by the course of Fate all evil from the bounds of His state. Wherefore if you look to the disposition of Providence, you will reckon naught as bad of all the evils which are held to abound upon earth.

BOETHIUS

But I see that now you are weighed down by the burden of the question, and wearied by the length of our reasoning, and waiting for the gentleness of song. Take then your draught, be refreshed thereby and advance further the stronger.

If thou wouldst diligently behold with unsullied mind the laws of the God of thunder upon high, look to the highest point of heaven above. There, by a fair and equal compact, do the stars keep their ancient peace. The sun is hurried on by its whirl of fire, but impedes not the moon's cool orb. The Bear turns its rushing course around the highest pole of the universe, and dips not in the western depths, and though it sees the other constellations sink, it never seeks to quench its flames in the ocean stream. In just divisions of time does the evening star foretell the coming of the late shadows, and, as Lucifer, brings back again the warming light of day. Thus does the interchanging bond of love bring round their neverfailing courses; and strife is for ever an exile from the starry realms. This unity rules by fair limits the elements, so that wet yields to dry, its opposite, and it faithfully joins cold to heat. Floating fire rises up on high, and matter by its weight sinks down. From these same causes in warm spring the flowering season breathes its scents; then the hot summer dries the grain; then with its burden of fruits comes autumn again, and winter's falling rain gives moisture. This mingling of seasons nourishes and brings forth all on earth that has the breath of life; and again snatches them away and hides them, whelming in death all that has arisen. Meanwhile the Creator sits on high, rules all and guides, king and Lord, fount an d source of all, Law itself and wise judge of justice. He restrains all that stirs nature to motion, holds it back, and makes firm all that would stray. If He were not to recall them to their true paths, and set them again upon the circles of their courses, they would be torn from their source and so would perish. This is the common bond of love; all seek thus to be restrained by the limit of the good. In no other manner can they endure if this bond of love be not turned round again, and if the causes, which He has set, return not again.

Do you see now,' she continued, what follows upon all that we have said?'

What is it?' I asked.

That all fortune is plainly good,' she answered.

How can that be?' said I.

Consider this,' she said: all fortune, whether pleasant or difficult, is due to this cause; it is for the sake of rewarding the good or exercising their virtue, and of punishing and correcting bad men: therefore it is plain that all this fortune which is allowed to be just or expedient, must be good.'

Yes,' I said, that is a true argument, and when I think of the Providence or Fate about which you have taught me, the conclusion rests upon strong foundations. But if it please you, let us count it among those conclusions which you a little while ago set down as inconceivable.'

Why?' she asked.

Because it is a commonplace saying among men -- indeed an especially frequent one -- that some people have bad fortune.'

Would you then have us approach more nearly the common conversation of men, lest we should seem to withdraw too far from human ways?'

If you will,' I said.

Do you not think that that, which i s advantageous, is good?'

Yes.'

And that fortune, which exercises or corrects, is advantageous?'

I agree,' said I.

Then it is good, is it not?'

It must be so.'

This is the fortune of those who are either firmly set in virtue and struggling against their difficulties, or of those who would leave their vices and take the path of virtue?'

That is true,' I said.

But what of that pleasant fortune which is granted as a reward to good men? Do most people perceive that it is bad? No; but, as is true, they esteem it the best. And what of the last kind of fortune, which is hard and which restrains bad men by just punishment? Is that commonly held to be good?'

No,' said I, it is held to be the most miserable of all that can be imagined.'

Beware lest in following the common conception, we come to some truly inconceivable conclusion.'

What do you mean?'

From what we have allowed,' she said, it results that the fortune of those who are in possession of virtue, or are gaining it, or advancing therein, is entirely good, whatever it be, while for those who remain in wickedness, their fortune is the worst.'

That is true, but who would dare confess it?'

For this reason a wise man should never complain, whenever he is brought into strife with fortune; just as a brave man cannot properly be disgusted whenever the noise of battle is heard, since for both of them their very difficulty is their opportunity, for the brave man of increasing his glory, for the wise man of confirming and strengthening his wisdom. From this is virtue itself so named, [65] because it is so supported by its strength that it is not overcome by adversity. And you who were set in the advance of virtue have not come to this pass of being dissipated by delights, or enervated by pleasure; but you fight too bitterly against all fortune. Keep the middle path of strength and virtue, lest you be overwhelmed by misfortune or corrupted by pleasant fortune. All that falls short or goes too far ahead, has contempt for happiness, and gains not the reward for labour done. It rests i n your own hands what shall be the nature of the fortune which you choose to form for yourself. For all fortune which seems difficult, either exercises virtue, or corrects or punishes vice.

The avenging son of Atreus strove for full ten years before he expiated in the fall of Phrygian Troy the wrong done to his brother's marriage. The same Agamemnon must needs throw off his father's nature, and himself, an unwilling priest, thrust his knife into his unhappy daughter's throat, and buy the winds at the cost of blood, when he sought to fill the sails of the fleet of Greece. The King of Ithaca wept sore for his lost comrades whom the savage Polyphemus swallowed into his huge maw as he lay in his vast cave; but, when mad for his blinded eye, he paid back with rejoicings for the sad tears he had drawn. Hercules became famous through hard labours. He tamed the haughty Centaurs, and from the fierce lion of Nemea took his spoil. With his sure arrows he smote the birds of Stymphalus; and from the watchful dragon took the apples of the Hesperides, filling his hand with their precious gold; and Cerberus he dragged along with threefold chain. The story tells how he conquered the fierce Diomede and set before his savage mares their master as their food. The Hydra's poison perished in his fire. He took the horn and so disgraced the brow of the river Achelous, who hid below his bank his head ashamed. On the sands of Libya he laid Antæus low; Cacus he slew to sate Evander's wrath. The bristling boar of Erymanthus flecked with his own foam the shoulders which were to bear the height of heaven; for in his last labour he bore with unbending neck the heavens, and so won again his place in heaven, the reward of his last work.

Go forth then bravely whither leads the lofty path of high example. Why do ye sluggards turn your backs? When the earth is overcome, the stars are yours.

---

[53] This and some of the following lines allude to some of the theories of the early Physicists.
[54] From Plato's Gorgias (466). Boethius in this and several other passages in this book has the Gorgias in mind; for Plato there discusses the strength and happiness of good men, and the impotence and unhappiness of bad men. Socrates is also there represented as proving that the unjust man is happier punished than unpunished, as Boethius does below.
[55] P. 84.

[56] Cf. St. Matthew x. 28.

[57] Plato, Gorgias, 472 and ff.

[58] It must not be supposed from the words cleansing mercy' (purgatoria clementia) that Boethius held the same views as were held by the Church later concerning purgatory, and as are now taught by the Roman Catholic Church. It is true that St. Augustine had in 407 A.D. hinted at the existence of such a state, but it was not dogmatically inculcated till 604, in the Papacy of Gregory the Great.

[59] Plato, Gorgias, 474 and ff.

[60] Arcturus, the star in Boötes nearest to the Bear, used to be thought the nearest star to our pole. Boötes was also known as the Arctophylax, or Bearward, and so also as the driver of the Wain.

[61] The old superstition was that an eclipse meant the withdrawal of the moon, and that by a noise of beaten brass, etc., she could be saved.

[62] Lucan, Pharsalia, i. 128. This famous line refers to the final triumph of Cæsar at Thapsus, B.C. 46, when Cato considered that the Republican cause was finally doomed and he committed suicide at Utica rather than survive it.

[63] The author is supposed to be Hermes Trismegistus, who wrote in the third century after Christ. The word powers' was used by many Neo-Platonic philosophers for those beings in the scale of nature, with which they filled the chasm between God and man. But Boethius does not seem to intend the word to have that definite meaning here.

[64] Homer, Iliad, xii. 176.

[65] The Latin word virtus' means by its derivation, manly strength.

BOOK V

HERE she made an end and was for turning the course of her speaking to the handling and explaining of other subjects. Then said I: Your encouragement is right and most worthy in truth of your name and weight. But I am learning by experience what you just now said of Providence; that the question is bound up in others. I would ask you whether you think that Chance exists at all, and what you think it is?'

Then she answered: I am eager to fulfil my promised debt, and to shew you the path by which you may seek your home. But these things, though all-expedient for knowledge, are none the less rather apart from our path, and we must be careful lest you become wearied by our turnings aside, and so be not strong enough to complete the straight journey.'

Have no fear at all thereof,' said I.' It will be restful to know these things in which I have so great a pleasure; and when every view of your reasoning has stood firm with unshaken credit, so let there be no doubt of what shall follow.'

I will do your pleasure,' she made answer, and thus she began to speak:

If chance is defined as an outcome of random influence, produced by no sequence of causes, I am sure that there is no such thing as chance, and I consider that it is but an empty word, beyond shewing the meaning of the matter which we have in hand. For what place can be left for anything happening at random, so long as God controls everything in order? It is a true saying that nothing can come out of nothing. None of the old philosophers has denied that, though they did not apply it to the effective principle, but to the matter operated upon -- that is to say, to nature; and this was the foundation upon which they built all their reasoning. If anything arises from no causes, it will appear to have risen out of nothing. But if this is impossible, then chance also cannot be anything of that sort, which is stated in the definition which we mentioned.'

BOETHIUS

Then is there nothing which can be justly called chance, nor anything "by chance"?' I asked. Or is there anything which common people know not, but which those words do suit?'

My philosopher, Aristotle, defined it in his Physics [66] shortly and well-nigh truly.'

How?' I asked.

Whenever anything is done with one intention, but something else, other than was intended, results from certain causes, that is called chance: as, for instance, if a man digs the ground for the sake of cultivating it, and finds a heap of buried gold. Such a thing is believed to have happened by chance, but it does not come from nothing, for it has its own causes, whose unforeseen an d unexpected coincidence seem to have brought about a chance. For if the cultivator did not dig the ground, if the owner had not buried his money, the gold would not have been found. These are the causes of the chance piece of good fortune, which comes about from the causes which meet it, and move along with it, not from the intention of the actor. For neither the burier nor the tiller intended that the gold should be found; but, as I said, it was a coincidence, and it happened that the one dug up what the other buried. We may therefore define chance as an unexpected result from the coincidence of certain causes in matters where there was another purpose. The order of the universe, advancing with its inevitable sequences, brings about this coincidence of causes. This order itself emanates from its source, which is Providence, and disposes all things in their proper time and place.

In the land where the Parthian, as he turns in flight, shoots his arrows into the pursuer's breast, from the rocks of the crag of Achæmenia, the Tigris and Euphrates flow from out one source, but quickly with divided streams are separate. If they should come together and again be joined in a single course, all, that the two streams bear along, would flow in one together. Boats would meet boats, and trees meet trees torn up by the currents, and the mingled waters would together entwine their streams by chance; but their sloping beds restrain these chances vague, and the downward order of the falling torrent guides their courses. Thus does chance, which seems to rush onward without rein, bear the bit, and take its way by rule.'

I have listened to you,' I said, and agree that it is as you say. But in this close sequence of causes, is there any freedom for our judgment or does this chain of fate bind the very feelings of our minds too?'

There is free will,' she answered. Nor could there be any reasoning nature without freedom of judgment. For any being that can use its reason by nature, has a power of judgment by which it can without further aid decide each point, and so distinguish between objects to be desired and objects to be shunned. Each therefore seeks what it deems desirable, and flies from what it considers should be shunned. Wherefore all who have reason have also freedom of desiring and refusing in themselves. But I do not lay down that this is equal in all beings. Heavenly and divine beings have with them a judgment of great insight, an imperturbable will, and a power which can effect their desires. But human spirits must be more free when they keep themselves safe in the contemplation of the mind of God; but less free when they sink into bodies, and less still when they are bound by their earthly members. The last stage is mere slavery, when the spirit is given over to vices and has fallen away from the possession of its reason. For when the mind turns its eyes from the light of truth on high to lower darkness, soon they are dimmed by the clouds of ignorance, and become turbid through ruinous passions; by yielding to these passions and consenting to them, men increase the slavery which they have brought upon themselves, and their true liberty is lost in captivity. But God, looking upon all out of the infinite, perceives the views of Providence, and disposes each as its destiny has already fated for it according to its merits: "He looketh over all and heareth all." [67]

Homer with his honeyed lips sang of the bright sun's clear light; yet the sun cannot burst with his feeble rays the bowels of the earth or the depths of the sea. Not so with the Creator of this great sphere. No masses of earth can block His vision as He looks over all. Night's cloudy darkness cannot resist Him. With one glance of His intelligence He sees all that has been, that is, and that is to come. He alone can see all things, so truly He may be called the Sun.' [68]

Then said I, Again am I plunged in yet more doubt and difficulty.'

BOETHIUS

What are they,' she asked, 'though I have already my idea of what your trouble consists?'

There seems to me,' I said, 'to be such incompatibility between the existence of God's universal foreknowledge and that of any freedom of judgment. For if God foresees all things and cannot in anything be mistaken, that, which His Providence sees will happen, must result. Wherefore if it knows beforehand not only men's deeds but even their designs and wishes, there will be no freedom of judgment For there can neither be any deed done, nor wish formed, except such as the infallible Providence of God has foreseen. For if matters could ever so be turned that they resulted otherwise than was foreseen of Providence, this foreknowledge would cease to be sure. But, rather than knowledge, it is opinion which is uncertain; and that, I deem, is not applicable to God. And, further, I cannot approve of an argument by which some men think that they can cut this knot; for they say that a result does not come to pass for the reason that Providence has foreseen it, but the opposite rather, namely, that because it is about to come to pass, therefore it cannot be hidden from God's Providence. In that way it seems to me that the argument must resolve itself into an argument on the other side. For in that case it is not necessary that that should happen which is foreseen, but that that which is about to happen should be foreseen; as though, indeed, our doubt was whether God's foreknowledge is the certain cause of future events, or the certainty of future events is the cause of Providence. But let our aim be to prove that, whatever be the shape which this series of causes takes, the fulfilment of God's foreknowledge is necessary, even if this knowledge may not seem to induce the necessity for the occurrence of future events. For instance, if a man sits down, it must be that the opinion, which conjectures that he is sitting, is true; but conversely, if the opinion concerning the man is true because he is sitting, he must be sitting down. There is therefore necessity in both cases: the man must be sitting, and the opinion must be true. But he does not sit because the opinion is true, but rather the opinion is true because his sitting down has preceded it. Thus, though the cause of the truth of the opinion proceeds from the other fact, yet there is a common necessity on both parts. In like manner we must reason of Providence and future events. For even though they are foreseen because they are about to happen, yet they do not happen because they are foreseen. None the less it is necessary that either what is about to happen should be foreseen of God, or that what has been foreseen should happen; and this alone is enough to destroy all free will.

Yet how absurd it is that we should say that the result of temporal affairs is the cause of eternal foreknowledge! And to think that God foresees future events because they are about to happen, is nothing else than to hold events of past time to be the cause of that highest Providence. Besides, just as, when I know a present fact, that fact must be so; so also when I know of something that will happen, that must come to pass. Thus it follows that the fulfilment of a foreknown event must be inevitable.

Lastly, if any one believes that any matter is otherwise than the fact is, he not only has not knowledge, but his opinion is false also, and that is very far from the truth of knowledge Wherefore, if any future event is such that its fulfilment is not sure or necessary, how can it possibly be known beforehand that it will occur? For just as absolute knowledge has no taint of falsity, so also that which is conceived by knowledge cannot be otherwise than as it is conceived. That is the reason why knowledge cannot lie, because each matter must be just as knowledge knows that it is. What then How can God know beforehand these uncertain future events? For if He thinks inevitable the fulfilment of such things as may possibly not result, He is wrong; and that we may not believe, nor even utter, rightly. But if He perceives that they will result as they are in such a manner that He only knows that they may or may not occur, equally, how is this foreknowledge, this which knows nothing for sure, nothing absolutely? How is such a foreknowledge different from the absurd prophecy which Horace puts in the mouth of Tiresias: "Whatever I shall say, will either come to pass, or it will not "? [69] How, too, would God's Providence be better than man's opinion, if, as men do, He only sees to be uncertain such things as have an uncertain result? But if there can be no uncertainty with God, the most sure source of all things, then the fulfilment of all that He has surely foreknown, is certain. Thus we are led to see that there is no freedom for the intentions or actions of men; for the mind of God, foreseeing all things without error or deception, binds all together and controls their results. And when we have once allowed this, it is plain how complete is the fall of all human actions in consequence. In vain are rewards or punishments set before good or bad, for there is no free or voluntary action of the mind to deserve them and what we just now determined was most fair, will prove to be most unfair of all, namely to punish the dishonest or reward the honest, since their own will does not put them in the way of honesty or dishonesty, but the unfailing necessity of development constrains them. Wherefore neither virtues nor vices are anything, but there is rather an indiscriminate confusion of all deserts. And nothing could be more vicious than this; since the whole order of all comes from Providence, and nothing is left to human intention, it follows that our crimes, as well as our good deeds, must all be held due to the author of all good. Hence it is unreasonable to hope for or pray against aught. For what could any man hope for or pray against, if an undeviating chain links together all that we can desire? Thus will the only understanding between God and man, the right of prayer, be taken away. We suppose that at the price of our deservedly humbling ourselves before Him we may win a right to the inestimable reward of His divine grace: this is the only manner in which men can seem to deal with God, so to speak, and by virtue of prayer to join ourselves to that inaccessible light, before it is granted to us; but if we allow the inevitability of the future, and believe that we have no power, what means shall we have to join ourselves to the Lord of all, or how can we cling to Him? Wherefore, as you sang but a little while ago, [70] the human race must be cut off from its source and ever fall away.

What cause of discord is it breaks the bonds of agreement here? What heavenly power has set such strife between two truths? Thus, though apart each brings no doubt, yet can they not be linked together. Comes there no discord between these truths? Stand they for ever sure by one another? Yes, 'tis the mind, o'erwhelmed by the body's blindness, which cannot see by the light of that dimmed brightness the finest threads that bind the truth. But wherefore burns the spirit with so strong desire to learn the hidden signs of truth? Knows it the very object of its careful search? Then why seeks it to learn anew what it already knows? If it knows it not, why searches it in blindness? For who would desire aught unwitting? Or who could seek after that which is unknown? How should he find it, or recognise its form when found, if he knows it not? And when the mind of man perceived the mind of God, did it then know the whole and parts alike? Now is the mind buried in the cloudy darkness of the body, yet has not altogether forgotten its own self, and keeps the whole though it has lost the parts. Whosoever, therefore, seeks the truth, is not wholly in ignorance, nor yet has knowledge wholly; for he knows not all, yet is not ignorant of all. He takes thought for the whole which he keeps in memory, handling again what he saw on high, so that he may add to that which he has kept, that which he has forgotten.'

Then said she, This is the old plaint concerning Providence which was so strongly urged Philosophy by Cicero when treating of Divination, [71] and you yourself have often and at length questioned the same subject. But so far, none of you have explained it with enough diligence or certainty. The cause of this obscurity is that the working of human reason cannot approach the directness of divine foreknowledge. If this could be understood at all, there would be no doubt left. And this especially will I try to make plain, if I can first explain your difficulties.

Tell me why you think abortive the reasoning of those who solve the question thus; they argue that foreknowledge cannot be held to be a cause for the necessity of future results, and therefore free will is not in any way shackled by foreknowledge. [72] Whence do you draw your proof of the necessity of future results if not from the fact that such things as are known beforehand cannot but come to pass? If, then (as you yourself admitted just now), foreknowledge brings no necessity to bear upon future events, how is it that the voluntary results of such events are bound to find a fixed end? Now for the sake of the argument, that you may turn your attention to what follows, let us state that there is no foreknowledge at all. Then are the events which are decided by free will, bound by any necessity, so far as this goes? Of course not. Secondly, let us state that foreknowledge exists, but brings no necessity to bear upon events; then, I think, the same free will will be left, intact and absolute. "But," you will say, "though foreknowledge is no necessity for a result in the future, yet it is a sign that it will necessarily come to pass." Thus, therefore, even if there had been no foreknowledge, it would be plain that future results were under necessity; for every sign can only shew what it is that it points out; it does not bring it to pass. Wherefore we must first prove that nothing happens but of necessity, in order that it may be plain that foreknowledge is a sign of this necessity. Otherwise, if there is no necessity, then foreknowledge will not be a sign of that which does not exist. Now it is allowed that proof rests upon firm reasoning, not upon signs or external arguments; it must be deduced from suitable and binding causes. How can it possibly be that things, which are foreseen as about to happen, should not occur? That would be as though we were to believe that events would not occur which Providence foreknows as about to occur, and as though we did not rather think this, that though they occur, yet they have had no necessity in their own natures which brought them about. We can see many actions developing before our eyes; just as chariot drivers see the development of their actions as they control and guide their chariots, and many other things likewise. Does any necessity compel any of those things to occur as they do? Of course not. All art, craft, and intention would be in vain, if everything took place by compulsion. Therefore, if things have no necessity for coming to pass when they do, they cannot have any necessity to be about to come to pass before they do. Wherefore there are things whose results are entirely free from necessity. For I think not that there is any man who will say this, that things, which are done in the present, were not about to be done in the past, before they are done. Thus these foreknown events have their free results. Just as foreknowledge of present things brings no necessity to bear upon them as they come to pass, so also foreknowledge of future things brings no necessity to bear upon things which are to come.

But you will say that there is no doubt of this too, whether there can be any foreknowledge of things which have not results bounden by necessity. For they do seem to lack harmony: and you think that if they are foreseen, the necessity follows; if there is no necessity, then they cannot be foreseen; nothing can be perceived certainly by knowledge, unless it be certain. But if things have uncertainty of result, but are foresee n as though certain, this is plainly the obscurity of opinion, and not the truth of knowledge. For you believe that to think aught other than it is, is the opposite of true knowledge. The cause of this error is that every man believes that all the subjects, that he knows, are known by their own force or nature alone, which are known; but it is quite the opposite. For every subject, that is known, is comprehended not according to its own force, but rather ac cording to the nature of those who know it. Let me make this plain to you by a brief example: the roundness of a body may be known in one way by sight, in another way by touch. Sight can take in the whole body at once from a distance by judging its radii, while touch clings, as it were, to the outside of the sphere, and from close at hand perceives through the material parts the roundness of the body as it passes over the actual circumference. A man himself is differently comprehended by the senses, by imagination, by reason, and by intelligence. For the senses distinguish the form as set in the matter operated upon by the form; imagination distinguishes the appearance alone without the matter. Reason goes even further than imagination; by a general and universal contemplation it investigates the actual kind which is represented in individual specimens. Higher still is the view of the intelligence, which reaches above the sphere of the universal, and with the unsullied eye of the mind gazes upon that very form of the kind in its absolute simplicity. Herein the chief point for our consideration is this: the higher power of understanding includes the lower, but the lower never rises to the higher. For the senses are capable of understanding naught but the matter; imagination cannot look upon universal or natural kinds; reason cannot comprehend the absolute form; whereas the intelligence seems to look down from above and comprehend the form, and distinguishes all that lie below, but in such a way that it grasps the very form which could not be known to any other than itself. For it perceives and knows the general kind, as does reason; the appearance, as does the imagination; and the matter, as do the senses, but with one grasp of the mind it looks upon all with a clear conception of the whole. And reason too, as it views general kinds, does not make use of the imagination nor the senses, but yet does perceive the objects both of the imagination and of the senses. It is reason which thus defines a general kind according to its conception: Man, for instance, is an animal, biped and reasoning. This is a general notion of a natural kind, but no man denies that the subject can be approached by the imagination and by the senses, just because reason investigates it by a reasonable conception and not by the imagination or senses. Likewise, though imagination takes its beginning of seeing and forming appearances from the sense s, yet without their aid it surveys each subject by an imaginative faculty of distinguishing, not by the distinguishing faculty of the senses.

Do you see then, how in knowledge of all things, the subject uses its own standard of capability, and not those of the objects known? And this is but reasonable, for every judgment formed is an act of the person who judges, and therefore each man must of necessity perform his own action from his own capability and not the capability of any other. In days of old the Porch at Athens [73] gave us men, seeing dimly as in old age, who could believe that the feelings of the senses and the imagination were but impressions on the mind from bodies without them, just as the old custom was to impress with swift-running pens letters upon the surface of a waxen tablet which bore no marks before. But if the mind with its own force can bring forth naught by its own exertions; if it does but lie passive and subject to the marks of other bodies; if it reflects, as does, forsooth, a mirror, the vain reflections of other things; whence thrives there in the soul an all-seeing power of knowledge? What is the force that sees the single parts, or which distinguishes the facts it knows? What is the force that gathers up the parts it has distinguished, that takes its course in order due, now rises to mingle with the things on high, and now sinks down among the things below, and then to itself brings back itself, and, so examining, refutes the false with truth? This is a cause of greater power, of more effective force by far than that which only receives the impressions of material bodies. Yet does the passive reception come first, rousing and stirring all the strength of the mind in the living body When the eyes are smitten with a light, or the ears are struck with a voice's sound, then is the spirit's energy aroused, and, thus moved, calls upon like forms, such as it holds within itself, fits them to signs without and mingles the forms of its imagination with those which it has stored within.

With regard to feeling the effects of bodies, natures which are brought into contact from without may affect the organs of the senses, and the body's passive affection may precede the active energy of the spirit, and call forth to itself the activity of the mind; if then, when the effects of bodies are felt, the mind is not marked in any way by its passive reception thereof, but declares that reception subject to the body of its own force, how much less do those subjects, which are free from all affections of bodies, follow external objects in their perceptions, and how much more do they make clear the way for the action of their mind? By this argument many different manners of understanding have fallen to widely different natures of things. For the senses are incapable of any knowledge but their own, and they alone fall to those living beings which are incapable of motion, as are sea shell-fish, and other low forms of life which live by clinging to rocks; while imagination is granted to animals with the power of motion, who seem to be affected by some desire to seek or avoid certain things. But reason belongs to the human race alone, just as the true intelligence is God's alone. Wherefore that manner of knowledge is better than others, for it can comprehend of its own nature not only the subject peculiar to itself, but also the subjects of the other kinds of knowledge. Suppose that the senses and imagination thus oppose reasoning, saying, "The universal natural kinds, which reason believes that it can perceive, are nothing; for what is comprehensible to the senses and the imagination cannot be universal: therefore either the judgment of reason is true, and that which can be perceived by the senses is nothing or, since reason knows well that there are many subjects comprehensible to the senses and imagination, the conception of reason is vain, for it holds to be universal what is an individual matter comprehensible to the senses." To this reason might answer, that "it sees from a general point of view what is comprehensible to the senses and the imagination, but they cannot aspire to a knowledge of universals, since their manner of knowledge cannot go further than material or bodily appearances; and in the matter of knowledge it is better to trust to the stronger and more nearly perfect judgment." If such a trial of argument occurred, should not we, who have within us the force of reasoning as well as the powers of the senses and imagination, approve of the cause of reason rather than that of the others? It is in like manner that human reason thinks that the divine intelligence cannot perceive the things of the future except as it conceives them itself. For you argue thus: "If there are events which do not appear to have sure or necessary results, their results cannot be known for certain beforehand: therefore there can be no foreknowledge of these events; for if we believe that there is any foreknowledge thereof, there can exist nothing but such as is brought forth of necessity." If therefore we, who have our share in possession of reason, could go further and possess the judgment of the mind of God, we should then think it most just that human reason should yield itself to the mind of God, just as we have determined that the senses and imagination ought to yield to reason.

Let us therefore raise ourselves, if so be that we can, to that height of the loftiest intelligence. For there reason will see what it cannot of itself perceive, and that is to know how even such things as have uncertain results are perceived definitely and for certain by foreknowledge; and such foreknowledge will not be mere opinion, but rather the single and direct form of the highest knowledge unlimited by any finite bounds.

In what different shapes do living beings move upon the earth! Some make flat their bodies, sweeping through the dust and using their strength to make therein a furrow without break; some flit here and there upon light wings which beat the breeze, and they float through vast tracks of air in their easy flight. 'Tis others' wont to plant their footsteps on the ground, and pass with their paces over green fields or under trees. Though all these thou seest move in different shapes, yet all have their faces downward along the ground, and this doth draw downward and dull their senses. Alone of all, the human race lifts up its head on high, and stands in easy balance with the body upright, and so looks down to spurn the earth. If thou art not too earthly by an evil folly, this pose is as a lesson. Thy glance is upward, and thou dost carry high thy head, and thus thy search is heavenward: then lead thy soul too upward, lest while the body is higher raised, the mind sink lower to the earth.

Since then all that is known is apprehended, as we just now shewed, not according to its nature but according to the nature of the knower, let us examine, so far as we lawfully may, the character of the divine nature, so that we may be able to learn what its knowledge is.

The common opinion, according to all men living, is that God is eternal. Let us therefore consider what is eternity. For eternity will, I think, make clear to us at the same time the divine nature and knowledge.' Eternity is the simultaneous and complete possession of infinite life. This will appear more clearly if we compare it with temporal things. All that lives under the conditions of time moves through the present from the past to the future; there is nothing set in time which can at one moment grasp the whole space of its lifetime. It cannot yet comprehend to-morrow; yesterday it has already lost. And in this life of to-day your life is no more than a changing, passing moment. And as Aristotle [74] said of the universe, so it is of all that is subject to time; though it never began to be, nor will ever cease, and its life is co-extensive with the infinity of time, yet it is not such as can be held to be eternal. For though it apprehends and grasps a space of infinite lifetime, it does not embrace the whole simultaneously; it has not yet experienced the future. What we should rightly call eternal is that which grasps and possesses wholly and simultaneously the fulness of unending life, which lacks naught of the future, and has lost naught of the fleeting past; and such an existence must be ever present in itself to control and aid itself, and also must keep present with itself the infinity of changing time. Therefore, people who hear that Plato thought that this universe had no beginning of time and will have no end, are not right in thinking that in this way the created world is co-eternal with its creator [75] For to pass through unending life, the attribute which Plato ascribes to the universe is one thing; but it is another thing to grasp simultaneously the whole of unending life in the present; this is plainly a peculiar property of the mind of God.

And further, God should not be regarded as older than His creations by any period of time, but rather by the peculiar property of His own single nature. For the infinite changing of temporal things tries to imitate the ever simultaneously present immutability of His life: it cannot succeed in imitating or equalling this, but sinks from immutability into change, and falls from the single directness of the present into an infinite space of future and past. And since this temporal state cannot possess its life completely and simultaneously, but it does in the same manner exist for ever without ceasing, it therefore seems to try in some degree to rival that which it cannot fulfil or represent, for it binds itself to some sort of present time out of this small and fleeting moment; but inasmuch as this temporal present bears a certain appearance of that abiding present, it somehow makes those, to whom it comes, seem to be in truth what they imitate. But since this imitation could not be abiding, the unending march of time has swept it away, and thus we find that it has bound together, as it passes, a chain of life, which it could not by abiding embrace in its fulness. And thus if we would apply proper epithets to those subjects, we can say, following Plato, that God is eternal, but the universe is continual.

Since then all judgment apprehends the subjects of its thought according to its own nature, and God has a condition of ever-present eternity, His knowledge, which passes over every change of time, embracing infinite lengths of past and future, views in its own direct comprehension everything as though it were taking place in the present. If you would weigh the foreknowledge by which God distinguishes all things, you will more rightly hold it to be a knowledge of a never-failing constancy in the present, than a foreknowledge of the future. Whence Providence is more rightly to be understood as a looking forth than a looking forward, because it is set far from low matters and looks forth upon all things as from a lofty mountain-top above all. Why then do you demand that all things occur by necessity, if divine light rests upon them, while men do not render necessary such things as they can see? Because you can see things of the present, does your sight therefore put upon them any necessity? Surely not. If one may not unworthily compare this present time with the divine, just as you can see things in this your temporal present, so God sees all things in His eternal present. Wherefore this divine foreknowledge does not change the nature or individual qualities of things: it sees things present in its understanding just as they will result some time in the future. It makes no confusion in its distinctions, and with one view of its mind it discerns all that shall come to pass whether of necessity or not. For instance, when you see at the same time a man walking on the earth and the sun rising in the heavens, you see each sight simultaneously, yet you distinguish between them, and decide that one is moving voluntarily, the other of necessity. In like manner the perception of God looks down upon all things without disturbing at all their nature, though they are present to Him but future under the conditions of time. Wherefore this foreknowledge is not opinion but knowledge resting upon truth, since He knows that a future event is, though He knows too that it will not occur of necessity. If you answer here that what God sees about to happen, cannot but happen, and that what cannot but happen is bound by necessity, you fasten me down to the word necessity, I will grant that we have a matter of most firm truth, but it is one to which scarce any man can approach unless he be a contemplator of the divine. For I shall answer that such a thing will occur of necessity, when it is viewed from the point of divine knowledge; but when it is examined in its own nature, it seems perfectly free and unrestrained. For there are two kinds of necessities; one is simple: for instance, a necessary fact, "all men are mortal"; the other is conditional; for instance, if you know that a man is walking, he must be walking: for what each man knows cannot be otherwise than it is known to be; but the conditional one is by no means followed by this simple and direct necessity; for there is no necessity to compel a voluntary walker to proceed, though it is necessary that, if he walks, he should be proceeding. In the same way, if Providence sees an event in its present, that thing must be, though it has no necessity of its own nature. And God looks in His present upon those future things which come to pass through free will. Therefore if these things be looked at from the point of view of God's insight, they come to pass of necessity under the condition of divine knowledge; if, on the other hand, they are viewed by themselves, they do not lose the perfect freedom of their nature. Without doubt, then, all things that God foreknows do come to pass, but some of them proceed from free will; and though they result by coming into existence, yet they do not lose their own nature, because before they came to pass they could also not have come to pass.

"What then," you may ask, "is the difference in their not being bound by necessity, since they result under all circumstances as by necessity, on account of the condition of divine knowledge?" This is the difference, as I just now put forward: take the sun rising and a man walking; while these operations are occurring, they cannot but occur: but the one was bound to occur before it did; the other was not so bound. What God has in His present, does exist without doubt; but of such things some follow by necessity, others by their authors' wills. Wherefore I was justified in saying that if these things be regarded from the view of divine knowledge, they are necessary, but if they are viewed by themselves, they are perfectly free from all ties of necessity: just as when you refer all, that is clear to the senses, to the reason, it becomes general truth, but it remains particular if regarded by itself. "But," you will say, "if it is in my power to change a purpose of mine, I will disregard Providence, since I may change what Providence foresees." To which I answer, "You can change your purpose, but since the truth of Providence knows in its present that you can do so, and whether you do so, and in what direction you may change it, therefore you cannot escape that divine foreknowledge: just as you cannot avoid the glance of a present eye, though you may by your free will turn yourself to all kinds of different actions." "What?" you will say, "can I by my own action change divine knowledge, so that if I choose now one thing, now another, Providence too will seem to change its knowledge?" No; divine insight precedes all future things, turning them back and recalling them to the present time of its own peculiar knowledge. It does not change, as you may think, between this and that alternation of foreknowledge. It is constant in preceding and embracing by one glance all your changes. And God does not receive this ever-present grasp of all things and vision of the present at the occurrence of future events, but from His own peculiar directness. Whence also is that difficulty solved which you laid down a little while ago, that it was not worthy to say that our future events were the cause of God's knowledge. For this power of knowledge, ever in the present and embracing all things in its perception, does itself constrain all things, and owes naught to following events from which it has received naught. Thus, therefore, mortal men have their freedom of judgment intact. And since their wills are freed from all binding necessity, laws do not set rewards or punishments unjustly. God is ever the constant foreknowing overseer, and the ever-present eternity of His sight moves in harmony with the future nature of our actions, as it dispenses rewards to the good, and punishments to the bad. Hopes are not vainly put in God, nor prayers in vain offered: if these are right, they cannot but be answered. Turn therefore from vice: ensue virtue: raise your soul to upright hopes: send up on high your prayers from this earth. If you would be honest, great is the necessity enjoined upon your goodness, since all you do is done before the eyes of an all-seeing Judge.'

[66] Aristotle, Physics, ii. 3.

[67] A phrase from Homer (Iliad, iii. 277, and Odyssey, xi. 109), where it is said of the sun.

[68] This sentence, besides referring to the application of Homer's words used above, contains also a play on words in the Latin, which

can only be clumsily reproduced in English by some such words as The sole power which can see all is justly to be called the solar.'

[69] Horace, Staires, II. v. 59.

[70] Supra, Book IV. Met. vi. p. 135.

[71] Cicero, De Divinatione, II.

[72] Referring to Boethius's words in Prose iii. of this book, p.145.

[73] Zeno, of Citium (342-270 B. C.), the founder of the Stoic school, taught in the Stoa Poekile, whence the name of the school. The following lines refer to their doctrine of presentations and impressions.

[74] Aristotle, De Cælo, 1.

[75] Boethius speaks of people who hear that Plato thought, etc.,' because this was the teaching of some of Plato's successors at the Academy. Plato himself thought otherwise, as may be seen in the Timæus, e.g. ch. xi. 38 B., Time then has come into being along with the universe, that being generated together, together they may be dissolved, should a dissolution of them ever come to pass; and it was made after the pattern of the eternal nature that it might be as like to it as possible. For the pattern is existent for all eternity, but the copy has been, and is, and shall be, throughout all time continually.' (Mr. Archer Hind's translation.)

A Note on the Translation

The present translation of THE CONSOLATION OF PHILOSOPHY' is the work of Mr. W. V. COOPER, B.A., King's College, Cambridge, who has thus carried on the tradition of English renderings of Boethius's famous work, the list of translators beginning with the illustrious name of Alfred the Great. The recent Millenary, celebrated at Winchester, has perhaps justified the issue of this first of twentieth-century versions. The Frontispiece, taken from an Elzevir Sallust printed in 1634, has been chosen by way of illustrating both the fortune of the author and his famous idea of the changeableness of Fortune's Wheel.

I. G. December 19, 1901.

APPENDIX

(See Book ll., Prose iii. p. 32)

BOETHIUS'S first wife was Elpis, daughter of Festus. The following epitaph has been handed down as that of Elpis, and has been said by some to have been written by Boethius himself: --

> Hope [76] was my name, and Sicily my home,
> Where I was nursed, until I came from thence
> An exile for the love I bore my lord:
> Apart from him my time was full of tears,
> Heavy the day, laden with care the night,
> (But with him all was joy and peace and love) [77]
> And now, my pilgrim's journey o'er, I rest
> Within this sacred place, and witness bear
> Before the throne of the Eternal Judge on high.

[76] Elpis is a Greek word meaning hope
[77] This line is lost from the original Latin.

BOETHIUS

he wrote those works, he combated Arianism during his life, and during his imprisonment he was engaged upon a treatise on the Unity of the Trinity, as well as upon this work. Here perhaps lies an explanation of what must seem strange to us at first sight, namely, that a Christian should apparently look to Philosophy rather than to his religion for comfort in persecution and support at the approach of death. But it is to be feared that in his day, and in the society in which he moved, Christianity meant to many who professed it little more than a subject for rivalry and argument among sects and for the combating of heresies. With many of the contemporaries of Boethius, therefore, a new book of comfort sought for in Christian doctrine would not have had much influence, and there seems to be no reason why people of our own day, even those who draw the greatest help from their religion, should not enjoy the additional comfort which solaced an honest and pious thinker in a time of apparently intolerable and incredible misfortune.

The wide learning of Boethius may be partly shewn by a list of some of his writings, which included original works and translations in many branches of study. For instance, he translated into Latin a great number of Aristotle's works on different subjects, such as those on Rhetoric, Logic, the Categories, etc. He translated three books of Euclid, and wrote other mathematical works. He translated and wrote books upon Music and Mechanics, and one upon Astronomy. His theological works included treatises against the Nestorians and Arians.

But his Consolation is the work upon which his fame rests. The veneration in which this book was held in the middle ages and onward is abundantly shewn by the numerous translations made of it. It was very early rendered into German, and later on translated into the French of the day by Jehan de Meun and others in later times; into Greek by Maximus Planudes, into Italian and Spanish. In England translations have appeared at intervals during the last thousand years. For just that space of time has passed since that noble educator of his people, Alfred the Great, translated it with Asser's help, thinking, it would seem, that this work was most worthy of his people's reading of all books after the Bible. But his version does not give us a very true knowledge either of Boethius or his Consolation. It is of the greatest value to the student of Alfred, because there are many indisputably genuine sayings and opinions of that wise man. There are wise thoughts upon kingly duty and many definitely Christian maxims. These were outside the theme of Boethius, though wise themselves and deeply interesting as Alfred's own work. Furthermore, the more abstruse parts are wholly omitted, probably as being of little use for King Alfred's subjects.

In later times that most versatile scholar, Queen Elizabeth translated it. Chaucer, Sir Thomas More, and Leslie , Bishop of Ross, the adviser of Mary, Queen of Scots, wrote imitations of it. Robert of Lincoln (Grosstête) commented upon it. In the sixteenth century appeared Colville's very fine translation. Translations in verse appeared in the seventeenth century by Harry Coningsby and Lord Preston; others followed in the eighteenth and nineteenth centuries. Its influence is to be found perhaps even in the oldest English poetry of pre-Conquest times; it is certainly very marked in Chaucer, Gower, Spenser, and many another later poet. And in Italy, Dante makes St. Thomas Aquinas point out the spirit of Boethius in Paradise with these words: --

> Now if thy mental eye conducted be
> From light to light as I resound their fame,
> The eighth well worth attention thou wilt see.
> Within it dwells, all excellence beholding,
> The soul who pointed out the world's dark ways,
> To all who listen, its deceits unfolding.
> Beneath in Cieldauro lies the frame
> Whence it was driven; from woe and exile to
> This fair abode of peace and bliss it came.'

Paradiso, x. 121 ff (Wright's translation.)

CHRONOLOGICAL TABLE A.D.

470. Anicius Manlius Severinus Boethius, born of most distinguished family.

470. Anicius Manlius Severinus Boethius, born of most distinguished family.

493. Theodoric, the Ostrogothic king, becomes sole master of Italy.

510. Boethius consul.

522. His two sons consuls, and Boethius distributes enormous largesses.

526. While using his influence as Theodoric's magister officiorum' for the purity of the government and the welfare of the Italians, Boethius was charged with treason. Without his being allowed to defend himself, his property was confiscated, and he himself condemned to death. He was imprisoned at Ticinum (Pavia), tortured, and brutally put to death at Calvenzano. His father-in-law, Symmachus, was also executed.

722. Liutprand, king of the Lombards, erected a tomb to his memory in the Church of S. Pietro Ciel d'Oro at Pavia. (See the quotation from Dante above.)

A few words on Theodoric may conclude this note.

Theodoric was born A.D. 455, educated at Constantinople as a hostage of the Emperor Leo, and succeeded his father as King of the Ostrogoths in 475. His youth was spent chiefly in war. He attacked his ally, the Emperor Zeno, in 487. To save Constantinople, Zeno gave him leave to expel Odoacer from Italy. Practically the whole Gothic nation migrated with Theodoric's army to Italy, where Odoacer was thrice defeated. He consented to allow Theodoric to reign jointly with him, but he was conveniently assassinated very soon afterwards, and Theodoric ruled till he died in 526, leaving the country certainly in a better state than that in which he found it, having ruled with moderation on the whole, and choosing good ministers such as Boethius. But in his last years he became influenced by unscrupulous men, informers, barbarian Ostrogoths, who oppressed the Italians, and the most bitter Arian sectaries, by each of which classes Boethius was hated as an honest and powerful minister, a protector of the oppressed Italians and as an orthodox Christian.

W. V. C.

Also from Benediction Books ...
Wandering Between Two Worlds: Essays on Faith and Art
Anita Mathias
Benediction Books, 2007.
152 pages
ISBN: 0955373700

Available from: www.amazon.com, www.amazon.co.uk
www.wanderingbetweentwoworlds.com

     In these wide-ranging lyrical essays, Anita Mathias writes, in lush, lovely prose, of her naughty Catholic childhood in Jamshedpur, India; her large, eccentric family in Mangalore, a sea-coast town converted by the Portuguese in the sixteenth century; her rebellion and atheism as a teenager in her Himalayan boarding school, run by German missionary nuns, St. Mary's Convent, Nainital; and her abrupt religious conversion after which she entered Mother Teresa's convent in Calcutta as a novice. Later rich, elegant essays explore the dualities of her life as a writer, mother, and Christian in the United States--Domesticity and Art, Writing and Prayer, and the experience of being "an alien and stranger" as an immigrant in America, sensing the need for roots.

About the Author

     Anita Mathias was born in India, has a B.A. and M.A. in English from Somerville College, Oxford University and an M.A. in Creative Writing from the Ohio State University. Her essays have been published in The Washington Post, The London Magazine, The Virginia Quarterly Review, Commonweal, Notre Dame Magazine, America, The Christian Century, Religion Online, The Southwest Review, Contemporary Literary Criticism, New Letters, The Journal, and two of HarperSanFrancisco's The Best Spiritual Writing anthologies. Her non-fiction has won fellowships from The National Endowment for the Arts; The Minnesota State Arts Board; The Jerome Foundation; The Vermont Studio Center; The Virginia Centre for the Creative Arts, and the First Prize for the Best General Interest Article from the Catholic Press Association of the United States and Canada. Anita has taught Creative Writing at the College of William and Mary, and now lives and writes in Oxford, England.

EDITORIAL NOTE

THE incompatibility of the sufferings of good men, the impunity and success of bad men, with the government of the world by a good God, has been a subject of thought among men ever since religion and abstract questions have occupied the thoughts of mankind. The poetical books of the Bible are full of it, particularly, of course the book of Job, which is a dramatic poem entirely devoted to the subject. The New Testament contains much teaching on the same question. Among the Greeks the tragedians and later philosophers delighted in working out its problems. But from the sixth to the seventeenth centuries of our era the De Consolatione of Boethius, in its original Latin and in many translations, was in the hands of almost all the educated people of the world. The author's personal history was well known. He was a man whose fortunes had risen to the highest pitch possible under the Roman Empire; who had himself experienced the utter collapse of those fortunes, and was known to have sustained himself through imprisonment and even to torture and an unjust death by the thoughts which he left to mankind in this book.

It is a work which appealed to Pagan and Christian alike. There is no Christian doctrine relied upon throughout the work, but there is also nothing which could be in conflict with Christianity. Even the personification of Philosophy, though after the form of a pagan goddess, is precisely like the Wisdom' of Solomon in the Apocrypha; and the same habit of thought led the Jews to personify the Word' of God, and use it as identical with God Himself; and the same led to that identifying of the Word' with Christ, which we find in the first chapter of St. John's Gospel. So, if there is nothing distinctly or dogmatically Christian in the work, there is also nothing which can be condemned as pagan, in spite of the strong influence of pagan philosophy, with which Boethius was intimate.

For though some have held that the Christianity of Boethius was foisted upon him, with his canonisation as St. Severinus, after his death by those who thought he must have been too good a man to have been a heathen, and though the authenticity of his theological works also has therefore been doubted, yet we may now be almost certain that he was a Christian, and an orthodox Christian, for if it is true that

CPSIA information can be obtained at www.ICGtesting.com
Printed in the USA
LVOW110809161012

303046LV00001B/18/P